The Leatherwood Civil War Letters

Letters Written by:
William H. Leatherwood, Joseph D. Leatherwood, and
Other Family Members

Members of the Union Army
Enlisted in the War of the Rebellion

Letters Transcribed by: **Lois Ellen Fenn**
Letter Curator: **Mary Hadley Frances**
Editor and compiler: **Joseph Dalton Leatherwood, Junior**

The Leatherwood Family in America Series
Volume XV

Third printing, 2019 (revised)
Fourth Printing, 2021 (revised)
The Leatherwood Family in America Series (Volume XV)

Library of Congress-in-publication

Leatherwood, Joseph Dalton, 1947-living

The Leatherwood Civil War Letters written by William H. Leatherwood, Joseph D. Leatherwood and Family. Members of the Northwestern Branch of the Leatherwood Family in America

Includes index

ISBN - 13: 978-0692971246

1 - Civil War Letters; 2 - Leatherwood family - genealogy; 3 - Genealogy Ohio Leatherwood family; 4 – Genealogy Joseph D. Leatherwood; 5 – Emily Pleasant Nichols family tree; 6 – Northwestern Leatherwoods – genealogy; 7 – Lois Ellen Fenn.

Front and back covers show a 25 March 1863 handwritten letter from William H. Leatherwood to his brother Joseph D. Leatherwood.

Published in the United States by: **The Leatherwood Family in America Series** (Volume XV)

Dedication

This collection of letters is dedicated to the memory of

Lois Ellen Fenn

Leatherwood Genealogist and Historian

She made it possible for all of us to enjoy the letters.

Author of

The Northwest Leatherwoods: A Family History (Unpublished)

"A Soldier cant see his destiny two hours ahead he cant tell when he wil get orders to go or where he wil go."

William H. Leatherwood
February 28, 1864

"If you could just stand by my side one moment you would see sights that would make your blood run cold, thousands of men camped ready to move to the deadly conflict, the long lines of wagons as far as the eye can reach. My heart sickens at the sight, war, war, everything wears a war like appearance. Near us is a large fort its huge guns frowning angrily out in every direction. O that the time may soon Come when there shall be no use for them."

Joseph D. Leatherwood
April 24, 1864

Preface
The Retrogression of Virtue

By Joseph Dalton Leatherwood

War is a terrible thing, but it is not the most terrible. War is totalitarian in its character, it is totalism on display for all to see with its raw power and its ability to kill and maim and terrorize and destroy. Nation warring against nation, peoples against peoples, and the great eternal struggle of mankind, namely, those allied with Providence to stand against the forces of the prince of darkness – himself. War has been mankind's natural state since his beginning; O we abhor it, we condemn it, but nonetheless we fight because we must, we revel in its glory, and we parade down the streets in our uniforms adored with metals marching to demonstrate our courage, our bravery, and our determinism (our patriotism) to stand up at the time our nation needs us most.

We abhor war's totalitarianism because no matter the tactics and stratagems employed, from the creative chaos of the irregulars to the precision of the most well-disciplined army; war consumes, *it is a taker*. It is a dark god, war, it takes lives, it makes the most beautiful and gentle among us and makes them dead, it takes the most innocent and places them upon the alter of sacrifice to be crushed not for the progress of mankind but his retrogression. For it is this purpose, it is this 'ideal,' if you will, for which the god of war fights - man's retrogression, man's fallen nature. The greater the retrogression of virtue, the darker becomes the god of war and the more fanatical and frightening becomes the sacrifice to appease its appetite - the total degradation of man and the debasement of life as we know it.

Stripped of all sentimentality, the god of war seeks to take humanity toward barbarism and fear, toward the cosmic function of tyranny robbing from humanity any vestiges of man's ideals about chivalry or man's humanity toward his fellow man. The god of war sets out to destroy what it considers man's silly notion about liberty by taking liberty. It takes from mankind all concepts about a fidelity to life making it meaningless among the carnage and butchery. And its ultimate drive is toward the regimentation of mankind's pursuit of happiness by destroying it with a necessary totalitarianism. This is war; this is war's objective - a perverse totalitarianism – total war.

The god of war riding above the battle space has but one ethic – no humanity. It is purely authoritarian in its vision of order – consuming people, resources, technology, and knowledge regimenting or correlating them into opposing forces for either 'aggression' or 'defense.' Once mobilized, the forces assume one of these banners of conflict. The ethic of war does not differentiate between the two, i.e., a force of aggression may be 'liberating' resources of another for its own use and, in the pursuit of this end (this objective), and the subjugation of the conquered people is deemed necessary.

Continuing this example within the pure theory of war, the god of war 'justifies' the act of 'liberation' and subjugation as necessary. The god of war's 'ethic,' and only ethic, is a total pragmatism where the end (the objective) is justified by the means, that is, the god of war overthrows humanity's notion of chivalry, rendering it obsolete. To those who defended against the aggressors, a total discrimination is carried out against them. They must either acquiesce to or resist the imperialism of the aggressor; acquiescence means reconstruction or reeducation; resistance means being hunted down and jailed or being shot. The discrimination is justified by a total deceit built on the propaganda schemes of the victors. At its zenith, within the pure theory of war, total war, the god of war becomes totalitarian, there is a total imposition, militaristic socialism, of its will upon humanity through its statism (governance) and its aggression turns into total reaction a total imperialism of its vision. The god of war riding high above the battle space seeks only one thing - total victory – total darkness. The ethic of the god of war is totalism – embodied in its pragmatism, deceit, authoritarianism, discrimination, and imposition - bringing with it death, mayhem, terror, and the annihilation of entire populations, communities, nations, and civilizations along with reason itself.

As people of common sense fully realize, war is a symptom, it is not a causal factor; something far worse is the cause. As stated above, 'war is a terrible thing, but it is not the most terrible thing,' the most terrible thing is fostering war through man's *retrogression of virtue*. Indeed, the 'ethic' of the god of war and the full notion of a pure theory of war manifest from and fights because of man's falling away from virtue.

When a nation abandon's God, hope is lost though they may not realize it at the time and charity increasingly becomes the purview of the State. Mankind loses faith in one of two ways. On the one hand, it embraces some form of legalism or ritualism for justification of certain actions and beliefs, thinking all the time that he is doing God's will. On the other, he chooses to abandon, reject God all together for other gods embracing them as 'scientific constructs' to justify his actions. Either direction leads man into a willful rebellion against God. When mankind enters into rebellion, he is declaring war against God, even when he thinks he is operating within God's will or acting within some 'scientific construct.'

Man's inhumanity to man is endless, it is like the bottomless pit for which all inhumanity is one day destined. It emanates from the desire for power and control over others. Seeking to control through force and fraud and by whatever means necessary, be it enslavement or terrorism, it has been with us since Adam's fall and will continue to plague mankind. It is the reprobate mind at work.

J.D.L. 2017

Table of Contents

Introduction

I.

What follows is an account of the Civil War from the perspective of four individuals. The primary perspective comes from William H. Leatherwood. He documents the war from the infantryman's perspective, the aching feet, sorry grub, fears, optimism, and frustrations associated with war. William H. Leatherwood was one of three sons offered up to the War Between the States by Aaron Leatherwood or "Pap" and Elizabeth Hamilton Leatherwood (who had passed away three years before the Civil War).

The other sons were Joseph D. Leatherwood and Samuel Leatherwood. William nor Samuel would survive the war. Samuel died after only four months service on 8 October 1861 in a camp hospital at Cheat Mountain, Virginia. Samuel served in Company E of the 24th Regiment, Ohio Volunteer Infantry. He was a Sergeant (NCO) in the unit. Sergeant Samuel Leatherwood's obituary reads as follows:

"Sergeant Samuel Leatherwood died October 8th, at 7 o'clock A.M., aged 22 years. he was born in Adams County, Ohio, near Locust Grove, and was a son of Aaron Leatherwood. He enlisted as a soldier, to fight in the present national struggle, on the 1st day of June, 1861, at Hillsboro, Ohio, under Capt. J. B. Hill.

The company to which he belonged was soon attached to the 24th Ohio Regiment, and sent to Western Virginia, where he served as a faithful soldier until stricken down by disease. He suffered greatly during his illness, (which was Typhoid fever) but bore his sufferings with great fortitude, never murmuring.

He was kind and obliging to all his fellow soldiers, thereby gaining the good will and esteem of the company, and indeed, I might say, of all who knew him. We, the members of the company, feel that we have lost a friend by the death of our fellow soldier. "May he rest in peace."

For the information of the friends and relatives of the deceased I will add, that he was taken sick on the 20th of August, owing to exposure while on scout. The Surgeon of the Regiment did everything in his power to restore his health, and he had so far improved at one time as to be able to leave his quarters, but was taken worse again, from which he never recovered. I saw him a short time before he died. He appeared to be suffering a great deal.

I spoke to him, but he did not recognize anyone. At times he would call some person named "William," (his brother, we supposed.) He died on the morning of the 8th - was buried in the evening, with religious ceremonies and with the honors of war.

His lasting resting place is on a beautiful slope on the east side of our encampment, on Cheat Mountain Summit, and at any time can be easily ascertained and identified.

His friends have the best wishes of the members of Co. I, and we all feel a deep sympathy for their untimely loss. MAC[1]

---

[1] "Obituary of Sergeant Samuel Leatherwood of Company I, 24th Ohio Regiment," **Highland Weekly News**, Hillsborough, Ohio, 24 Oct 1861 Vol. XXV No.26, p. 2.

According to Lois Fenn, "As a little girl, my mother Tammie heard her aunts talk of Sam, their happy and mischievous brother and of how 'Cheat Mountain cheated them.'"[2]

II.

William Hamilton Leatherwood served in Company E of the 91st Regiment, Ohio Volunteer Infantry.[3] In her history, *The Northwestern Leatherwoods*, Lois Fenn wrote:

"On 8 August 1862, less than a year after Sam's death, Aaron's youngest son Will enlisted in the Ohio Volunteer Infantry. He also was stationed in the mountains of Virginia, in the area which soon became West Virginia. His letters ... reflect a very-routine army life with little adventure. But Will had a lively interest in people and affairs, and his letters are not dull. At one time, when the "copperhead" Vallandingham was running for the governor ship of Ohio, Will took his own straw vote of his company, and was quite disgusted with the number of men who were for "Val." But he was gratified to note that nearly all the Adams County boys were in favor of the opponent, a strong Union supporter.

"In August 1863, Will wrote a teasing letter to Joe, referring to an incident in early July which became the subject of family story-telling for long afterward. On July 4 the Confederate Morgan ... crossed the Ohio into eastern Indiana, turned east, and swept across southern Ohio in a nuisance raid, taking horses, guns, and food as he went. At the Leatherwood home, some of his men took Aaron's best saddle horse "Trim," frightened the girls and made them angry by taking "Pap" (Aaron, aged 56) as well as Joe down the road at an uncomfortable pace. They were soon released, but Joe followed for a while -- keeping carefully out of sight. Will's company later helped round up Morgan's Confederates after his capture - in southeastern Ohio. In his August letter, Will says: 'Well Jo I recon you dont want to soldier any more when old Morgan is in command he drills new recruits rather hard I shouldent like to be under him myself he did play hob generaly but he is done now for a while I couldant help langhing when I heard how they got you drawn in. I can imagine how you felt when they made you give up your gun but that was nothing if they had only left Trim. You run a risk and a grait one following them if they had got you again you would have went up the spout... '

"Will's spelling is highly original and punctuation very scarce, but his clear even handwriting shows careful training in his country school.

"The last letter in the collection was written at the end of February 1864. On 9 May 1864, an inferior force of Confederates attacked at Cloyd's Mountain, West Virginia, but was defeated and their General mortally wounded. The Union force won, but Corporal William Leatherwood was killed in the battle; to the home folk in Adams County there was no victory.

"In several letters Will had urged Joe not to enlist; he was the only son left to help their father, and he had a wife and small family now. (Will always sent loving messages to 'Willy and Tammy,' and baby Anna had also joined the family in 1862.) Evidently Joe had been thinking the problem over as the war grew longer and more bitter; on the day after the date of Will's last letter, before it could have reached him, he enlisted in the Second Ohio Volunteer Cavalry, and was mustered into service 9 March 1864. "He had a little vest-pocket dairy for the year 1864, in which entries begin on leap-year day when he listed. There are three spaces on each small page,

---

[2]   Lois Ellen Fenn, *The Northwestern Leatherwoods: A Family History*, unpublished family history, Page 17.

[3]   The 91st Regiment of the Ohio Volunteer Infantry was organized on September 7, 1862 to serve three years. It served until June 24, 1865. John Turley of Scioto County was the Colonel and Benjamin F. Coates of Adams County was the Lt. Col.

room for brief jottings only. He entered notes about letters written and those received from Emily, his sisters, and his sister-in-law Tam Newlon; one gets the feeling that these were more important than details of the war. But he mentions movements of his unit, places where they camped, etc., so that by referring to "Battles and Leaders of the Civil War" and similar books, it is possible to follow Joseph Leatherwood through the last year of the War. The Adjutant General's certificate names the battles in which his regiment took part. "Half a dozen letters, as well as the little diary, show that his part in the war was a matter of conscience, a job to be done, no matter how detestable. His early letters, before he was in uniform, describe new scenes at Erie, 'like a blue mountain covered with snow' and the view from the hills above the Potomac, 'one of the finest views I ever saw.' But from the hills he also saw army camps, lines of supply wagons, fortifications with huge guns 'frowning angrily out in every direction.'

"On the way to Washington the regiment had camped near Annapolis, where Joe gave his civilian coat to an old Negro; when the men were later ordered to send civilian clothes home or give them to the government on receiving uniforms, he wished the old Negro could have his pants, too. He spent the first afternoon in Washington visiting the Capitol, 'went all over it or nearly so. It is one of the finest things in this world, I wish you could see it.' The Washington letter closes with a fatherly admonition to the little ones at home: 'Well Tammy and Willy, pappy is well and hopes his little children are well, it pleases pappy to hear that you think about him and talk about him, he wants you to be good children, mind what mother says to you. You must not be saucy to Grandpap and the girls you must go to school and learn to read and write so you can write to pappy. You must not fight nor quarrel but be pretty children, take good care of Puss and Jack and old Bird till pappy comes home. (Jack was the family dog, and Bird a gentle old horse.)

"Joe was at Charles City Court House on the southward march when he 'received letter from Sister that Brother was dead.' That was on June 14, more than a month after Will was killed. Every letter from home seems to be noted in the diary; without comment, that carries the feeling of homesickness throughout the year.

"Joe enlisted in a cavalry regiment, but for most of the year 1864 the Second Ohio was listed as Dismounted Cavalry. One wonders how this differed from the infantry? It was just about the time of his leaving home that Grant was called to command the Union forces. So, during the spring and summer of 1864, the Second Ohio was slogging along in Grant's 'Jug Handle' campaign through Virginia, when Grant vowed 'to fight it out along this line if it takes all-summer.' Evidently the Ohio men were on the left, or east, of the Army of the Potomac as it moved south. Several entries in the diary mention 'heavy fighting on the right,' and the Adjutant General's certificate names several engagements at eastern points along the army's route.

"After terrible losses at Cold Harbor in the early days of June, Grant realized that he was not to take Richmond very soon, and he ordered 100,000 men (including the Ohio units under Gen. Harrison Wilson) to move on south of Richmond in order to cut lines of supply from the south. While the main force dug in near Petersburg for a siege of trench warfare, that was to last nine months, Wilson's men -- strengthened to a force of 5,000 -- were ordered to cut the rail lines. They moved fast. One account says, 'Wilson was absent ten days, marched 300 miles, and destroyed 60 miles of railroad and much valuable rolling stock.' He had lost a thousand men before he rejoined the cavalry corps at Lighthouse Point on July 2. There they remained nearly three weeks, recuperating from sixty days of marching, fighting, and almost incredible labor.

"At an inspection of Wilson's command, soon after its return, the Corps Inspector was struck by the variety of costumes. Some of the men were literally in rags from too intimate acquaintance with bush and brier, but they were in good spirits. One fine looking specimen of the American volunteer, whose arms and brasses were very bright, paraded in a pair of trousers barely covering his knees, and barefooted. 'Have you no shoes or stockings?' demanded the astonished inspecting officer. 'No, sir!' replied the man with a grin. 'Not this side of Ohio.'

"Joe leatherwood survived Wilson's Raid, but he came out of it with an injury of his right leg which caused him to limp for the rest of his life. His division and another were moved to northern Virginia in July to help defend Washington. Joe was given light duty because of his injured leg and from August 12 to the end of the month he was in hospital at Camp Stoneman near the Capital.

"Gen. Sheridan had taken command of the Army of the Shenandoah, and Wilson's men followed him in 'scorched earth' raids of the Valley. Joe's record shows that he was at the Battle of Winchester (scene of Sheridan's celebrated ride), and jottings in the diary indicate that as late as December his outfit was still mopping up along the Valley. Farmers like Joe could not have enjoyed burning barns and fields, even in the name of war.

"The little diary began with the last day of February, 1864. So, Joe wrote in a few 1865 dates on the earlier pages, recording some movements in February and April which follow the history of Sheridan's part in the closing weeks of the war. From the upper Shenandoah his divisions were ordered to the Richmond area, while Grant led a larger force against Petersburg, which finally fell; then Richmond. Lee moved west, but there was no hope for his army, and he met Grant at Appomattox.

"Joe's diary says, 'Left Petersburg April 27,' indicating that Wilson's men were among those helping to restore order in the fallen strongholds. The latest entries show this part of the army moving west along the southern border of Virginia. By June 20, when Joe wrote to Emily from Benton Barracks, he was in Missouri, hopefully awaiting discharge. Perhaps it was partly the let-down after fighting; but he makes it very clear that Missouri was not at all to his liking. He was stationed for a while at Rolla, later at Springfield; then, on 12 October 1865, Sergeant Joseph Leatherwood was at last discharged at Benton Barracks."[4]

III.

Little did Will and Joe know that one-hundred and sixty years later their letters would give us an insightful look at the "history" of the war. These letters were transcribed by Lois Ellen Fenn and preserved by Mary Sue Hadley Francis. Lois was the granddaughter of Joseph D. Leatherwood and Emily Pleasant Nichols Leatherwood. Lois' mother was Tamzen Sue Leatherwood and the Reverend Francis William Fenn. Tamzen Sue Leatherwood was the oldest child and daughter of Joseph D. Leatherwood. She is referred to in the letters as 'Tam." Mary Sue Hadley Francis is the great-granddaughter of Joseph D. Leatherwood. Mary's parents were Kathryn Ramona Leatherwood and Cornelius N. Hadley. Mary Sue had these letters and I wrote her in 1989 asking if I could get a copy of the

---

[4]   *Ibid*, pages 18, 19 and 20.

letters "...written during the Civil War to Joe by his brother Will, and by Joe to his wife, Emily and one from Emily to Joe."

Leatherwoods and those researching the Leatherwoods are grateful for both for their foresight; Lois - for investing the time to transcribe the letters - and Mary Sue Francis for saving them for posterity's sake. There are five parts to this book.

The first reproduces the letters written by William H. Leatherwood to Joseph D. Leatherwood. One handwritten letter from William Hamilton Leatherwood to his brother Joseph is included for 25 March 1863.

Part II reproduces the letters written by Joseph D. Leatherwood to Emily P. Leatherwood, his wife. There is one letter in Part II from Enos U. Newlon written from Knoxville, Tennessee to Emily Nichols Leatherwood, his aunt. There is one handwritten letter from Joseph D. Leatherwood to Emily Nichols Leatherwood, his wife, for 20 Jun 1865.

Part III reproduces two letters. The first was written in 1891 by Joseph D. Leatherwood. The subject of the letter was family matters including the settlement of his father's estate back in Ohio and his desire to talk with his son Will. Joseph D. Leatherwood had journeyed back to Ohio to settle his father's estate (Aaron Leatherwood) and take care of other matters. It is a revealing look at Joseph's "returning home" and the things he observes while in Ohio. The second letter is from a William A. Leatherwood who outlines the Leatherwood family history as he knew it. This is one of the most cited letters in Leatherwood history because it was one of the first attempts to posit a genealogy for the Leatherwood family in America. The handwritten letter from William A. Leatherwood to Joseph D. Leatherwood is included in this section.

Part IV provides the reader with a short synopsis of each unit Samuel, William and Joseph Leatherwood served in during the "War of the Rebellion." Part V of this book presents the Civil War letters as transcribed by Lois Ellen Fenn, that is, copies of her type written transcriptions. Part VI outlines the genealogical record for Joseph D. Leatherwood and his descendants. His genealogy is presented as the survivor of the war.

IV.

The letters point to several universal characteristics of the soldier no matter who they are, where they are or period of time as they relate to any war. The soldier, the editor speaking from experience, looks forward to each day more so if there is the possibility of letters coming from home. It gives the soldier great optimism someone somewhere is thinking about them and thinks enough of them to write.

Second, letters and news from home were more important to the soldier than what they were doing. Nothing gave them more pleasure than a letter from home and this is referred to in almost every letter in this collection. William and Joseph both asked the recipients to write about anything, as often as possible and told recipients their letters were never boring.

Third, you see men at war - accepting their plight, as it is. Yes, there were complaints and hardships, but their complaints dealt with the officer corps, the conduct of the war or the ill-temperate behavior of their comrades in arms (see especially the letter of Joseph of June 28, 1865). While the soldier may complain about the hardships, the duty, they accept it so long as there is purpose and results from their efforts. They could deal with their own condition that is why they accepted it as a given and something to be dealt with. It did not matter about the duty; it was what they had signed up for and it is what they would do and accept as part of their volunteering to serve.

Fourth, home sweet home was and is the most paramount thing on the minds of the soldier. This is made abundantly clear by the letters written by both of these men. Letters took their minds away from the routine and the fury of war and put them in another place – home – but for a fleeting moment. Understandably, one can discern a feeling of homesickness in almost every letter in the collection. Faith, family, and friends were very important, and they asked relations to pray for them and their comrades. They were concerned about family and wrote every relative they could get an address for. They wanted to know about friends who might be in other units so they might visit with them, pray for them, or keep up with their actions.

Fifth, and finally, politics was very important. After all, they were serving in the ultimate political action – the soldier is the point of the spear, the instrumentality of the State being used and directed to wage war against their fellow man. William's letters were very pointed when it came to politics there was no mistaking, he was a Republican and a stalwart supporter of the Union.

His letter of December 28, 1862 was very sharp in his belief about the war. After hearing about Burnside's defeat (Fredericksburg) and the subsequent flow of rumor and propaganda through the ranks about "Southern acknowledgement" and "comprymise," he states categorically, "I dont look at it that way yet. I would like to be at home verry well but I would rather do the fighting and then come [home]." There can be no doubt about his feelings concerning the war and the need to win the war.

V.

There has been no attempt to edit for spelling or grammar (word usage). As Lois Fenn noted above, the writing and spelling were highly original while the punctuation was very scarce. The letters have been left in their natural state (as transcribed) except for three things.

First, sentences have been shortened or parsed – particularly those that were obvious run-on sentences. Shortened does not mean cutting words, no words have been cut. All words in the originals – transcribed by Lois Fenn – are in the text. The changes in this area were to cut run –on sentences. It should be noted some sentences could not be parsed or shortened, these were left intact whether they made sense or not to protect the integrity of the letters. Second, paragraphs have been broken out where there were clear and obvious breaks in ideas and subjects. The changes make the letters easier to read and add perspective.

Third, some punctuation has been added, primarily commas. Military units were properly cited, instead of 117 or 91, the editor made them the 117th or the 91st.

The letters were optically scanned and then checked against the original copies (those transcribed by Lois Fenn) after they were converted by optical character recognition (OCR) into text. At every step of the way, the editor has tried his best to maintain and preserve the historical integrity of the letters.

The editor believes their historical significance speaks to the period and the time and are a testament to the perseverance of the Leatherwood family and the nation demonstrating the family's role in helping build this nation. The editor hopes the readers read and learn from the letters. I, as a descendant of the South Carolina Branch and a son of the South, was raised up in the land of rebel yells, confederate icons and never considered there might be anything like a Yankee Leatherwood. Well, here is the proof in the pudding, confirming the saying that the Civil War saw 'brother fight against brother.' Samuel, William and Joseph fought in and around the same areas where many of their Southern Leatherwood cousins also fought.

While we must all thank Lois Ellen Fenn, now deceased, and Mary Sue Hadley Francis for their work and contributions, I want the readers to know if there are mistakes they are the fault of the editor and not the transcriber or the curator.

Joseph D. Leatherwood, Jr.
Bulverde, Texas 2021

Pedigree Chart for Samuel Leatherwood

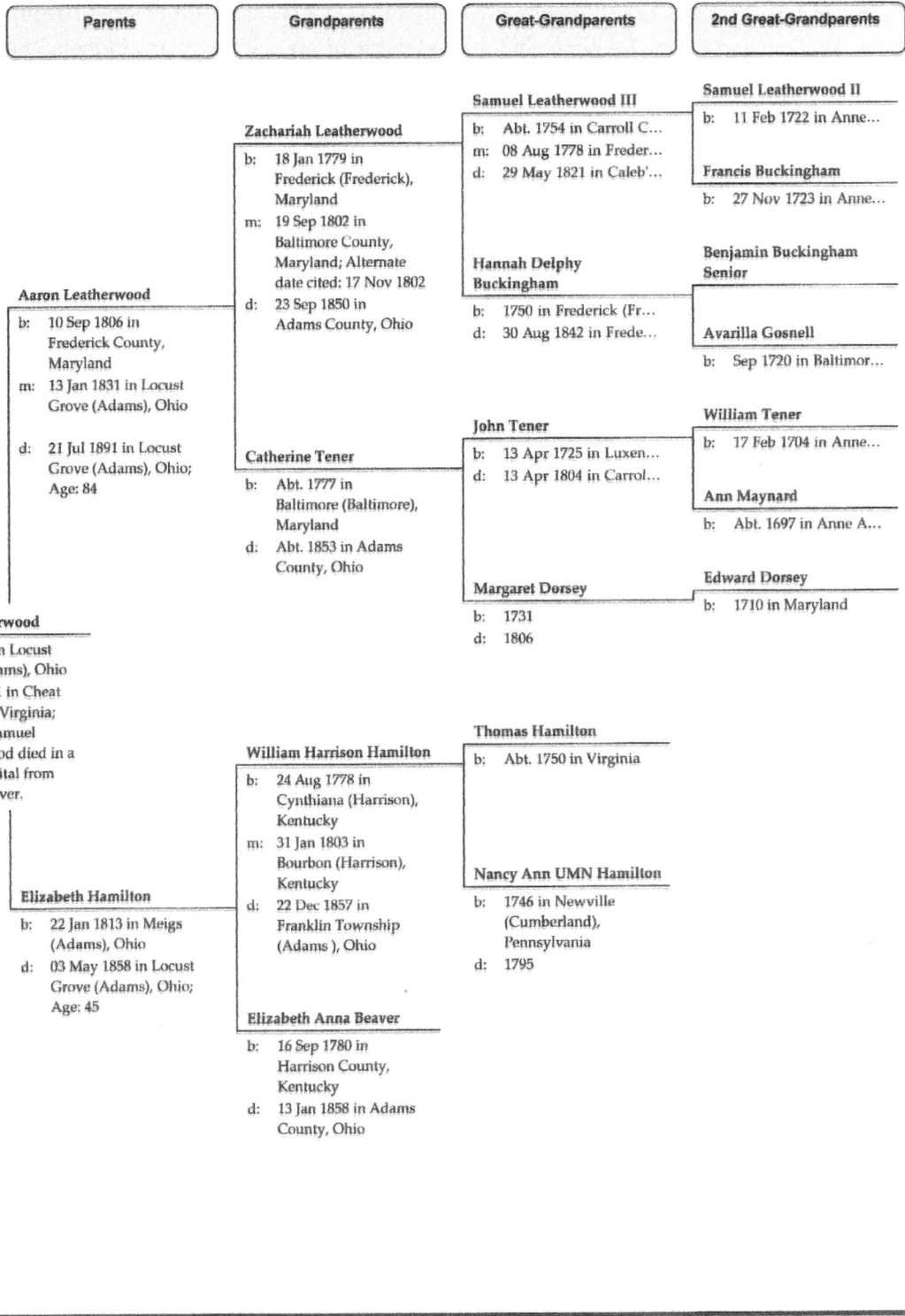

	Parents	Grandparents	Great-Grandparents	2nd Great-Grandparents

Samuel Leatherwood
b: Abt. 1838 in Locust Grove (Adams), Ohio
d: 08 Oct 1861 in Cheat Mountain, Virginia; Sergeant Samuel Leatherwood died in a camp hospital from Typhoid fever.

Parents

Aaron Leatherwood
b: 10 Sep 1806 in Frederick County, Maryland
m: 13 Jan 1831 in Locust Grove (Adams), Ohio
d: 21 Jul 1891 in Locust Grove (Adams), Ohio; Age: 84

Elizabeth Hamilton
b: 22 Jan 1813 in Meigs (Adams), Ohio
d: 03 May 1858 in Locust Grove (Adams), Ohio; Age: 45

Grandparents

Zachariah Leatherwood
b: 18 Jan 1779 in Frederick (Frederick), Maryland
m: 19 Sep 1802 in Baltimore County, Maryland; Alternate date cited: 17 Nov 1802
d: 23 Sep 1850 in Adams County, Ohio

Catherine Tener
b: Abt. 1777 in Baltimore (Baltimore), Maryland
d: Abt. 1853 in Adams County, Ohio

William Harrison Hamilton
b: 24 Aug 1778 in Cynthiana (Harrison), Kentucky
m: 31 Jan 1803 in Bourbon (Harrison), Kentucky
d: 22 Dec 1857 in Franklin Township (Adams), Ohio

Elizabeth Anna Beaver
b: 16 Sep 1780 in Harrison County, Kentucky
d: 13 Jan 1858 in Adams County, Ohio

Great-Grandparents

Samuel Leatherwood III
b: Abt. 1754 in Carroll C...
m: 08 Aug 1778 in Freder...
d: 29 May 1821 in Caleb'...

Hannah Delphy Buckingham
b: 1750 in Frederick (Fr...
d: 30 Aug 1842 in Frede...

John Tener
b: 13 Apr 1725 in Luxen...
d: 13 Apr 1804 in Carrol...

Margaret Dorsey
b: 1731
d: 1806

Thomas Hamilton
b: Abt. 1750 in Virginia

Nancy Ann UMN Hamilton
b: 1746 in Newville (Cumberland), Pennsylvania
d: 1795

2nd Great-Grandparents

Samuel Leatherwood II
b: 11 Feb 1722 in Anne...

Francis Buckingham
b: 27 Nov 1723 in Anne...

Benjamin Buckingham Senior

Avarilla Gosnell
b: Sep 1720 in Baltimor...

William Tener
b: 17 Feb 1704 in Anne...

Ann Maynard
b: Abt. 1697 in Anne A...

Edward Dorsey
b: 1710 in Maryland

Part I.

The Civil War Letters of William Hamilton Leatherwood to his brother Joseph D. Leatherwood

91ST REGIMENT OHIO VOLUNTEER INFANTRY

A Pedigree Chart for
William H. Leatherwood

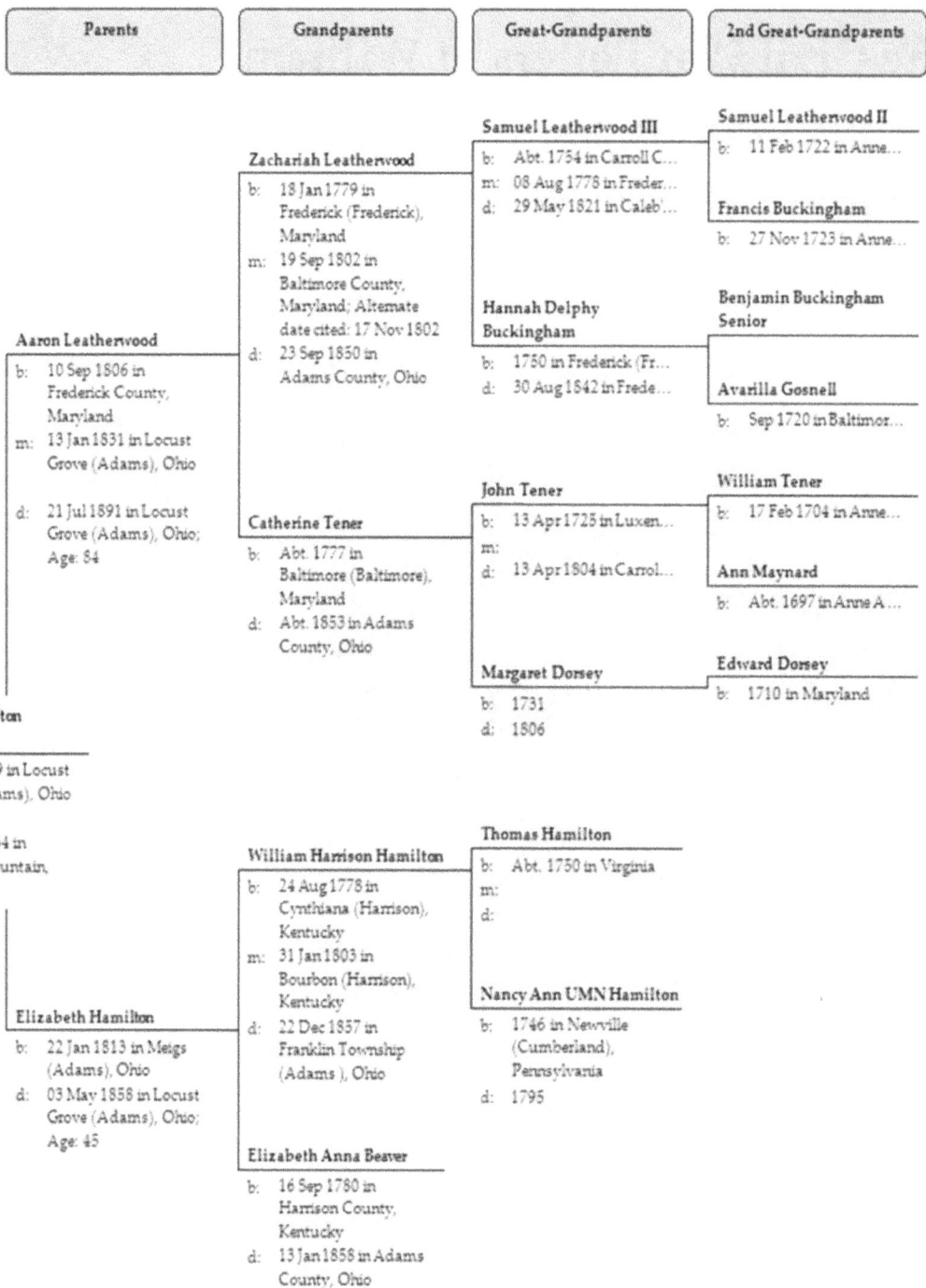

	Parents	Grandparents	Great-Grandparents	2nd Great-Grandparents

Samuel Leatherwood III
b: Abt. 1754 in Carroll C...
m: 08 Aug 1778 in Freder...
d: 29 May 1821 in Caleb'...

Samuel Leatherwood II
b: 11 Feb 1722 in Anne...

Zachariah Leatherwood
b: 18 Jan 1779 in
    Frederick (Frederick),
    Maryland
m: 19 Sep 1802 in
    Baltimore County,
    Maryland; Alternate
    date cited: 17 Nov 1802
d: 23 Sep 1850 in
    Adams County, Ohio

Francis Buckingham
b: 27 Nov 1723 in Anne...

Hannah Delphy Buckingham
b: 1750 in Frederick (Fr...
d: 30 Aug 1842 in Frede...

Benjamin Buckingham Senior

Avarilla Gosnell
b: Sep 1720 in Baltimor...

Aaron Leatherwood
b: 10 Sep 1806 in
    Frederick County,
    Maryland
m: 13 Jan 1831 in Locust
    Grove (Adams), Ohio
d: 21 Jul 1891 in Locust
    Grove (Adams), Ohio;
    Age: 84

Catherine Tener
b: Abt. 1777 in
    Baltimore (Baltimore),
    Maryland
d: Abt. 1853 in Adams
    County, Ohio

John Tener
b: 13 Apr 1725 in Luxen...
m:
d: 13 Apr 1804 in Carrol...

William Tener
b: 17 Feb 1704 in Anne...

Ann Maynard
b: Abt. 1697 in Anne A...

Margaret Dorsey
b: 1731
d: 1806

Edward Dorsey
b: 1710 in Maryland

William Hamilton Leatherwood
b: 07 Sep 1839 in Locust
    Grove (Adams), Ohio
m:
d: 09 May 1864 in
    Cloyd's Mountain,
    Virginia

William Harrison Hamilton
b: 24 Aug 1778 in
    Cynthiana (Harrison),
    Kentucky
m: 31 Jan 1803 in
    Bourbon (Harrison),
    Kentucky
d: 22 Dec 1857 in
    Franklin Township
    (Adams), Ohio

Thomas Hamilton
b: Abt. 1750 in Virginia
m:
d:

Nancy Ann UMN Hamilton
b: 1746 in Newville
    (Cumberland),
    Pennsylvania
d: 1795

Elizabeth Hamilton
b: 22 Jan 1813 in Meigs
    (Adams), Ohio
d: 03 May 1858 in Locust
    Grove (Adams), Ohio;
    Age: 45

Elizabeth Anna Beaver
b: 16 Sep 1780 in
    Harrison County,
    Kentucky
d: 13 Jan 1858 in Adams
    County, Ohio

20 August 1862 - Camp Portsmouth

Dear Brother,

I am still well. I got a little tuch of cold last night. It comes my time to stand gard to night, there was one gard run off last night, they put him on gard and he set his gun down and sloped. The Captain told me a little while ago that there was thirteen hundred men in camp. Well Jo, I was not as bad board as some of the boys thought I was in the Captain. He is second to none, he is no military man but he is as clever a man as I ever seen and is well thought of by all. We are looking for the Mustering Officer today.

My feet are getting verry sore, my boots are to tight for mustering in. I dont know how long we will stay here. I wish you would gow down to the Grove and tell Sam Teener[5] that I want him to make me a pare of boots, he has my measure. If you have any way of sending them down, you can find out whether any one is coming down or not, you had bettor not send down by the male for I never get to go out to town and it is so far out to camp that it would be a hard chance to get them, there is no telling how long we will stay here.

I would like for you to come down if you can. We have almost every thing gowing on here, some pray, some sing, some sware and som play cards. Tell the girls that I have not got my uniform yet but as soon as I get it I will have my miniture taken and send it to them. But I must come to a close, tell Tammy and Willy that I would like to see them. Nothing more at present but remain your afectionate bother W.H. Leatherwood.

Rite and let me know how the folks are getting along, direct to 91st Reg. OVI Camp Portsmouth, Ohio, care of Captain Clark.

---

[5] **Transcriber's note**: Sam Teener, mentioned above, was what my mother used to call "a sort of cousin," several Teeners who were nephews of her great-grandmother having moved to Ohio from Maryland about the time her great-grandparents Zachariah Leatherwood and Catherine (Teener) Leatherwood did. - L.E.F.

11 September 1862 - Camp Ironton

Dear Brother,

It is with pleasure that I take my pen to let you know that I am well at present.

Well I will begin by telling you my adventuers, we have been to Western Virginia and seen some of the efects of war. We got a dispatch that Old Jenkins was coming to Guyandott with about two thousands of men, we gathered up and started, there was six companies went up. We started night before last, we got up there just at day brake but the Rascals had left. There was Six Companies of the Second Virginia Cavalry there and as shure as you live they are a hard set of Boys but there is fight in them.

It is a hard looking place, it showes the efects of war, the houses are burnt and the people look distressed. We wer on small rasions while we was there, the Cavalry boys laughed at us for not gowing and taking what we wanted, they say they have learned to take care of themselves. We was only there about ten hours then we came back. Jenkins was in Barbersvill seven miles up the Guyan River. Colonel Turly dident want to gow with the armes we have and I suppose that was the reson that we came back, we are to get better arms today and then we will be apt to leave here.

I rote Pap a letter the other day about my money, I sent it to West Union to the Bank. Him or you must go and get it, if you want any of it you are welcom to it.

Well Jo I dont want to brag but when we got orders to march I was the first in ranks, the Boys comensed taring around asking questions and the Cap had hard work to get them in. It is not agreable to fight but Jo I am not afraid to fight and Jo acording to your request I am trying to be a good boy. I have had a good deal of enjoyment since I came in camp, you may rest satisfied conserning me.

Tell Em that I would like to see her but to tell the truth I would rather see Tamm and Willy than any body else, some times it seems to me that I would give amost any thing to see them. But I must come to a close, tell the folks that I am still on hand. I dont know where I will be when I wright again but let me be where I will my trust is in God. Jo remember me in your prayrs I expect this will be the last letter I will write here but I will write again soon. You must wright and tell me how you are getting along. Nothing more at present but remain your afectionate brother until death

William H. Leatherwood

21 September 1862 - Point Pleasant, Va.

Dear Brother,

It is with the gratest of pleasure that I take my pen this Sabbath mornin to let you know that I am well and harty. I received your letter on Wednesday and was glad to hear from home, nothing givs me more pleasure than a letter from home.

We are still here but have had no fight and not much prospect of it just now. We left Ironton on last Saturday week and I thought that I was gowing home, we started for Maysvill, we got the news that it was taken by a considerable force of Rebles. We all thought that we were gowing home to fight but alas we were all disapointed, we only got as far as Portsmouth and then got the fun of gowing back and a little further back than I agreed for I nawrly hate these poor Virginia hills, but here we are and cant help it.

We thought that we would have to march to Bufalow when we got here but thank Providence we dident. We had a hard trip up here, we had to lay on the hericon deck[6] and you had better believe it was som hot thru the day and not so hot at night as to pail? (peel) the hide. We got off of the Boat about noon on Sunday last and I was just sick enough to go and lay down in the shade, laying in the hot sun on the Boat gave me the headache but as soon as I got a drink of good watter I got better and today I feel as stout as a buck.

We have lots of company, there are seventeen Regiments here, there are three Batteries of artillery and I guess about two Regiments of cavalry.

Well Jo I am getting along with the Boys verry well, I have got in as good a mess as there is in the Company, the Boys came pretty ny having a dispute about who should have me.

I would have rote sooner but I could not get paper, it is not home here I just have to write as the case will admit of.

I was out on picket night before last but it is a thing I dont much hanker after it. This is a hard place the people are pretty nere all secesh but I think again we leave here they will vote the Union ticket. The farm our camp is on belongs to a Reble he is in the Reble army. If we stay here a while longer he maby will find his land if he gets back but that will be all. There is a man on the farm that says he is Union, he raised corn but we are gathering it. The cavalry boys pitch in and take the hard corn and we take the rostenears. We have got it about cleared out. We use the fence for cooking, the boys don't forget to catch the chickens, they caut the last old hen this morning and she had three little chickens. Colonel Turly says go ahead, he is rite.

Well Jo I will tell you about our grub, sometimes we get pretty good and sometimes it is hard, we got some beef the other day that was sort of how come you so and that wasent the first. But dont think I am disatisfied I am better satisfied than I have ever been. Captain D___y[7] give the quartermaster a cussing yesterday for not getting better grub for his men.

---

[6] **Transcriber's note**: Hurricane Deck?
[7] **Transcriber's note**: Captain's name is not clear.

Your letter encouraged me verry much you said to look ahead, I have always don that if I had have looked back I would have been dead be for now. I cant help thinking of home and if it was not for home I would have nothing to encouriage me and if I ever get into a fight and think of home the Rebles had better be agowing.

I could not help laughing when I read about Old Jacob gowing to make them git, I was sow surprised to here that Dock was Captain but I was glad that the people down in old Adams were a waking up to a sense of there duty. There is gowing to be somthing don, we got the news last evening that McClen had whiped Lee and taken Fifty thousand prisinors. If that is true I think that it will play out after a while. I showed the Captain your letter and he was much pleased with it, he said it was worth reading, he said if it hadent bin that some of the other Boys wanting to get off he would have give me a transfer to Murphys Company. I would have like very well to have been with them but I have friends here.

Jo I am still trying to live rite, I have to watch myselfe verry close for there are all most erry thing to draw the mind off but I am still on the way. I was sorry to here that the Boys that went to the Sixtieth Regiment wer taken prisinors, I am afraid that there Six months will turn out to be a long one.

Tell the Friends that I would like to write to all of them but it is impossible for me to do so, it is not like sitting down at home to rite a letter. I am under an Aple tree laying rite flat down with a barl head for a desk. But I must corne to a close by saying that I wish you all well and hope that we will all meet once more. Give my respects to all enquiring friends, tell Tammy and Willy that Uncle Will wants to see them, tell Em that I send my love to her. Direct your letters to Gallapolice Ohio nothing more at present, but remain your bother.

William H. Leatherwood
Gallipolis

8 October 1862 - Point Pleasant, Va.

Dear Brother,

It is with the gratest of pleasure that I take my pen to let you know that I am well this morning. I received your letter yesterday and are verry glad to here from you we have made a little move since I last rote. We have cosed (crossed) the Kanawba River. We was camped rite between the Ohio and the Kanawba, we are now on the south of the Kanawha. We are now in a Briggade the fourth and thirteenth Va. the thirty fourth and 91st Ohio, comanded by Col. _____.[8] The General is Gilmore. Well Jo I have got over my scare that I got up at Bufalow.

I was glad to here that you making the bulls git, just pitch into them. If I was at home I would like to have a company of bulls if I dident make them trot it would be curious. There is a considerable force here and more acoming there will be soething done in western Va. before long.

Jo I tell you I dont like the ide of wintering in these hills but if the rest can stand it Billy can. I am as harty as ever I was but it is not on acount of the fine things that we have to eat. We have had no soft Bread only what we bought. We have crackers and baken rice and beans and some beef that we captured at
Buffalow but I can do very well as long as I keep well I can go it.

You said you was not gowing to sow any wheat until it raind, if things look there like they do here I dont think you will, not some day soon for it is wonderful dry here but you have enough to do you anyhow.

Well I dont know how soon the war will be over but I hope it will be over in time for me to get home next winter. Jo we have as good an old Colonel as any other Reg. in the service. He haint above sneaking to any of us. You wanted to know the letter of our Co. it is Co. E. I fancy I could see you setting down making bulets to shoot the devlish Rebles but I must close you must wright if you cant rite much rite a little it dose me good to here from home if it haint but three words. Tell Em I am still the same Billy I think of little Tammy and Willy evry day. Recolect the letter is E, 91 Reg. nothing more at pesent but remain yours as ever

William Leatherwood.

---

[8] **Transcriber's note**: name not given.

5 November 1862 - Gauley Bridge, Va.

Dear Brother,

It is with grate pleasure that I rite you a few lines to let you know how I am getting along. The Lord is blessing me with excelent helth. I am growing fat on hard crackers baken and beens. I got your letter yesterday and it was a welkem visitor. It was with me like it was with you I hadent got any letter for some time but I wasent uneasy I knowed there was some acoming.

We have the pleasure of staying here at Gauley on the hill side. It is some of a job to get wood and watter. It is snowing to day but I am in the tent verry well satisfied to let it snow. You said that you felt for the soldiers. I dont doubt that but I havant suferd much since I have been out. I havent stood guard for over a month. I was on fatigue duty once. I am verry well off for cloths. I have two pare of pants and two woolon shirts overcoat dress coat blouse two pare of good socks and one not so good. I bought me a pare of gloves (sheep skin) of the host kind grait long fellows. My boots are good yet.

I was glad that you rote some war news. That is sonthing we dont get much on. I let some of the boys read it. They said it was good we all try to beleive one item in it that was that the war will be over soon. I supose the Boys of the Sixtieth are glad they are alive. Well I dont begrudge them the pleasure of home. The news of the change of Burnside and Rosecrans. We think that the war will close that much sooner.

We will move soon we will go to Fayetteville it is about fifteen miles from here over Cotten Mountain. We are good to winter in the hills. The 117th has got a good place. There are a heepe of barking here from cold it sounds distressing to wake up on a night and heer the coffing. We lay on the ground I have some cold but none to hurt. Well Billy would like to go home and stay about two weeks but he dont let that trouble his mind much.

Jo I am getting along with the Boys verry well. I havent saw a woman for some time. you must not think that I dont write to you. I write evry week. I dont want any thing from home without it is your prayers. If you can I would like to have some postage stamps send only a few at a time. I must close for the present write soon. Tell Enos Newland to tell me how he liked it. Tell the boys that I haint homesick yet. Tell Em and the girls that I send my love to them and I wouldent forget Pap and the little children. I would like to see you all. I still remain yours.

Will Leatherwood

19 November 1862 - Gauley Bridge, Va.

Well Jo I am here at Galley at last and it is a hard place. I am well all to my back. I got it hurt and I will tell you how I done it. I was detailed to guard the Battoes[9] [5] with provisions and the hands all left and I had to stay and work and pushing on them I hurt it but it will be all rite in a day or too. I was away from the Reg. fifteen days and when I came to camp the boys made as big a fuss as tho I had bin gone a month but I will pass.

I got yours and Cates letters and was glad to here from home. I have not riten as often as I would like to have done. I never got to Gauley until mondy. It is a hard looking place as soon as the sun gets up it begins to go down. I dont think we will stay all winter. I think we will go farther up or down there are a lot of soldiers in the Valley. We are comanded by General Scammon. We never here of the Rebles any more. A news paper is a rarity here.

You wanted to know what kind of guns we have. We have the Austrian Rifel. They shoot well. We have Caps and you wanted to know how I was fixed when that night it snowed. I was at a little Creek called Pokey. We made a sort of a shelter but I got wet and tuck a bad cold but it dident hurt me much. Them old Dankers are a getting mity fresh I should like to here of them being taken down.

You wanted to know whether I wanted any thing. I have no use for money for there is nothing to bye if I had plenty of it. Still have some I want you to write whether you got my money or not if you can. I would like if you would send me some Postage Stamps.

I must close. Tell Em that I send my love to her and the children. I believe that is all at present. I remain yours as ever.

Billy to Joseph Leatherwood

---

[9] **Transcriber's note**: Battoes - small flat-bottomed river boats (bateaux).

28 December 1862 - Fayetteville, Va.

Dear Brother,

This pleasent Sabbath day finds me seated in a nice cabin. I have just come off of guard. I was out on picket but dident get to see nary Reble. I was on the out post. It is pretty hard to stand on the out post. We are not alowed to sleep any. I got pretty sleepy last night.

I am well and harty. It is as nice a day as ever I saw for this time in the year. We have got our winter quarters done at last. If they let us stay here this winter, we will have a good time of it.

Well Jo the news are rather discouraging here. I hardly know how to take it. You know that I never believed any thing till the last pinch, but Old Burnside is wiped and no mistake. Some of the boys are getting verry much discouraged. They say we will never whip the Rebles. It does look rather spurious. Some of then say they would like to here that they had comprymise so they would get to go home. They would rather go home than save there country. I dont look at it that way yet. I would like to be at home verry well but I would rather do the fighting and then come.

The Boys are getting Furlows. I dont know whether I will get one or not. I believe if I can get one for twenty days I will come home. It would not give me much time to stay but if I only stay a week it would be verry much satisfaction to me. But I dont flatter my self with the idea of one but after some of the maried men get them I will stand as good a chance as any of them.

The pay master has not come yet we are looking for him soon. If he comes and I get a furlow I would be in town. They are beginning to make out the pay rolls then Uncle Sam will owe us four months pay. It would cost me about ten dollars to come home. I would freely give it just to see you all I would give that just to see the children. This is the dogondest place that ever I saw. There is hardly any buddy lives here and what does are the meanest people that ever the lord let live. They cant look at a man. It is here like it allways is, they just let them come in and go out just as they please almost buti must close. Write soon and often give my love to all

Yours truly Billy to Joseph Leatherwood

5 January 1863 - Fayetteville, Va.

Dear Brother,

Well Jo, your letter has just come to hand. I was glad to here from you that you were well but was sorry to here that you had the dumps so, but you must not let it get you down. So it may be that it will all work out rite yet. I knew that them Democrats would get sassy after the election. I am as hard on them as ever but it wont do to talk about that here. I am like old John Keesling, I think that if trators was cleaned out in Ohio that the war would close sooner.

To tell you the truth, I dont expect, if I live, to come home for three years that is to stay the way things look now we stand a good chants to stay out three years and then volunteer again. I know one that wont go again. I did think for a while that the thing would stop some time but I wouldent say now how long it would last.

We here some of the biggest news that you ever herd the boys are all getting tired of it. They are all complaining, Jo it is my opinion that this war will never be closed honerable. I have an idea that the Southern Confederacy will acknowledge at Iast. Well Jo I am some like you I think until we get better officers we will never gain the day. I still think that Old Abe means well but he is in a tite place.

There was awful news here about Burnsides defeat. I never know how to take any thing when I here it in short to tell you what I think of it I think it in a bad egg. I am not home sick yet but I do think it could be managed better I am getting along very well.

The Boys are very good to me and the officers are also good to me. Our Old Colonel cant be beat. He is clever and kind to his men but Old Scammon is a real old scoundrel. He makes the Boys take there hats off when they meet him. I have never had the honor of that though. I have ben on gard at his quarters.

You said that the 117th was steeling. If the Goverment will only send them up here they never will be disbanded for steeling for they couldent find any thing to steel.

That young Aston is a deserter. He left when we started from the Point. He had bettor keep scarce or he will be fetched back and it wont be so funney as gowing home was.

Jo you said that you dident know whether your letter would interest me or not. You may rest easy about that just give me plenty of such. Any thing from home dose me good. I never think of such a thing as desertion, it has plaid out with me but I am gowing to stick to it till the last cat is hung.

Jo I am sorry that you have to lose your rights. I think that Old Ned has payd # the rascal out and out. If there is any of my money left, you take it and use it. We are looking for the paymaster and then I will send you some more. You are as welcome to it as if it was your own. We will never quarI about it.

There are still some of the boys gowing home. I dont know whether I will get to come home or not. If the pay master dont come it will be hard for me to make the tri. There is no dificulty in a citizen coming here. There is some comes from Adams here. You could come to Piat on a boat. Camp Piat twenty five miles below the bridge then it is twelve miles here. The trains are gowing all the time to Piat.

If you think of coming up, I want you to let me know. If I dont get to come home, I will pay your way. If you will come it will only cost about ten dollars to come and go here.

I must tell you about the dreme I had last night I drempt that I saw Willy but I thought he was a corpse. I felt bad over it untill I got your letter to day. Language can not tell how well I would like to see them. It dose me good to here that they have not forgot me yet. I was sorry to here that James McClure was dead but we must all die one day or an other.

I must close soon you must write as often as you can dont think you will worry my pacience writing so much, write about every thing. I will not know for a month or so whether I will get to come home or not, then I will write to you and if you can come up I would be glad that is if I cant come home it will pay you to come and see the country. I believe that is all I can think of now so I will close by saying that I wish you all well. I send my love to you all yours in love.

     William Leatherwood

I will send your letters without paying the postage then you need not send so many I only want some to send a letter to some one else.

16 February 1863 - Fayetteville, Va.

Dear Brother,

Once more I take my pen to inform you that I am well. I received your letter on Saturday and on Sunday I had to go on guard so I could not answer it sooner. I was glad to here from you.

There is a hi old time here today the pay master has been here and payed us off and the Boys are lyting out like sheep. There was thirty or forty of the thirty fourth Boys went since Saturday there several of the twelfth and some of the ninty first, they are gowing evry chance they get it looks like the war would stop some time when all the soldiers desert then I guess it will stop.

I had a visitor last week. It was old Sammy Dempsy one of his sons is in the second Va. Cavlry and he come up to see him and he came in to our camp to see me. He says he thinks the war will stop about June or July. I hope it will.

Jo you spoke of gowing to the Army, you just stay at home as long as you live. If you haint forsed to go it is no fun and you just stay there. The Boys in the 117th are playing hob they will be a little carful how they do it after this.

You have had more snow down there than we have had up here. We have had rite smart rain. The mud is verry deep. I just came off guard this morning. Our company went after the deserters but they wont get any of them. There is two companyes out of our Regiment to look after them. There is two companies gon to Summers Ville to guard provisions and clothing. It is thirty five miles up Gauley above the Bridge, we are getting scatterd rite smart.

There is strong talk of our Regiment beeing mounted. If we are then we will see service. We are gowing to get new guns. We are gowing to get the Springfield Rifels then when we get an old poor horse then we will cut a big hog in the Ass, for my part it dont suit me verry well but it pleases me verry well that we are gowing to get new guns. The ones we have are not much account. They shoot like all the world but they dont shoot with any certanty. We have hard bread and pork that is two or three years old, beens have played out but we are fat yet.

Well I told you that the pay master had been here and payed us off. I got just forty nine dollars and I owed the Butler four dollars and sent thirty five home. I have eleven and a quarter left. We all sent our money with the pay master to Columbus and you can get it at West Union. I will send the receipt in this letter and you or Pap I had it put in his name but he can go to the County Auditor and he will give you an order to the County Tresurer and he will give you the money. That was the onley way we had to send it and it is as safe as any. If the receipt gets miscarried the Captain has it to show that I did send it and I can get it still. If you want any of it take it and use it. You are welcom to it go as soon as this comes to hand and get it. I asked Dempsy about it, he sayed it was safe.

Well I guess that is all now. You just stay at home if you know when you are well. I would like to see you but I have come to the conclusion that it wont pay you to come up here. You couldent have much satifaction. Well I guess that I have told you all that I can think of this time. So I will have to close. You must write soon and tell me whether you got this or not. Tell Em that I haint forgot her yet. Tell the folks must write soon and tell me whether you got this or not. Tell Em that I haint forgot her yet. Tell the folks that I am allrite yet and have no notion of deserting. I send my respects to all the friends and love to all the family. No more but remain your brother and friend

       William Leatherwood[10]
       Direct to Fayetteville, Va. Co. E, 91 Regiment

---

[10]   **Transcriber's note**: William Hamilton Leatherwood was promoted to Corporal on February 23, 1863.

25 March 1863 - Camp Reynolds, Va.

Dear Brother,

Once more I take my pen to let you know that I am well at present. I received your letter on the twenty first and was glad to here that you wer all well. We are camped on the bank of the Kanawha River just below the falls. It is a nice place far more so than where we was but I dont know how long we will stay here.

There is two Companies at Summers Ville and there is two more gowing to the Bridge and there is talk of some more gowing to loop Creek. I expect …

that ours will go next. The 91st will soon be no Regiment at all. It was counted the best Regiment in the Service from Ohio at least old Davis Tod says so. It has the most men for service than any other. The River is verry high today we have but little news here and I expect it is for the better.

I was glad to here that my receipt had got home. I was a little afraid it would not go safe. I saw in one of the County papers where Pap had got the Money.

Well, Jo, I must tell you what I think of the Conscript, I think it is …

all right. I have an idea that it will make som of them Secesh git up and dust. It is a verry tight law as you sayd but not any to tight for some. It has encouraged me some. Some of the Boys sayd that it would make war at home but I never thought so. If it was to, I would like for Co. E to go to Adams to help it along. Lieutenant Croford has returned, he says the People are more reconsiled than they was, he is well again. The Boys done a good job at Columbus.

The talk is that the Rebles are leaving Vixburg. If they let them run …

off I dont know what ought to be done with them but anything to keep the war gowing on. I am anxious to here of something being done. I do hope that the people at home will do the thing that is right and the war will be over a graideel sooner but I am gowing to write to Cate.

I will have to close this. I want you to rite as often as you can and give me the news of the day.   Give my Love to Emily and the Children. No more but remain your Loving Brother

W. H. Leatherwood

7 May 1863 - Summers Ville, Va.

Dear Brother,

This morning I take the opportunity of informing you where I am. We are at Summersville. We left Camp Reynolds Sunday the third and got here the fourth. I was so sore and tierd that I could not write. I am well. We made thirty two miles in one days time. I was one of the first in. We are getting farther from home and closer to the Rebs. There is no telling when we will have a fight here but they will find the 91st here when they come.

Jo I would rather be at home helping plant corn this morning. Sunday night I laid on the wet ground and it rained in my face. It made me mad we had to wade several Creeks. In fact it haint any fun to be a Soldier. This looks more like living than any place we have been for six months but there haint hardly any boddy lives here and nothing hardly to live on. I hardly think we will stay here verry long and of corse dont know where we will go. We may go to Clarksburg or down the Valley.

The Cavlery went out to Louisburg the other day and as usal they herd they was comming twenty four hours before. They got there and they was prepared for them and licked them out. The news goes here rite fast to the Rebs but none to us. They are all Rebles here they know anything quicker than we do. If I had my way about it I would kill evry devvle of them then we could do something.

The Regiment is all here, there is good brest works here for Infantry we have no Artilery here just Rifle pits. If they dont fetch Artilery here we will give them some fun.

I cant write much now as I have to write with a pencil on my knee. I dont know whether you can read this or not but if we stay here I will write you one. You can read. This is to let you know that I am alive. If I had a good place to write and a pen and ink I would give you a full description of the march and the country but I will do that when I get home. But to close tell Em, Tammy and Willy that Uncle Will still thinks of them and would like to see them. I give my love to all the family still direct to Charleston nothing more this tile still remaining yours as ever.

W. H. Leatherwood

15 May 1863 - Gauley Bridge Va.

Dear Brother,

Well, Jo, this morning I take my seat on the ground with my paper on my knee to write you a few lines. I am seated on the hill side above the Bridge. I as well I wrote to you when we was at Summerville but it was only a few lines. We got up there on the fourth and started back on the ninth so that our stay was short. It was a hard march up there and harder coming back. We made thirty two miles in thirteen hours.

I hardly know what was the idea for going up there without it was to have an excuse to hall a lot of grub up there for the Rebles to get. We was ordered away and everything there and when we got here there was two trains ordered up to get the grub and only a part of a company of Cavelry to guard it and the Rebles was wide awake and they waited untill the train got evry thing and started back and they pitched in captuerd the hole thing. The most of the Cavelry got away one Lieutenant and some of the men wer taken. It was the biggest Roar that ever I herd of. It looks to me like old Scammon just sent it up for the Rebs. If they had burnt up evry thing and the town they would not have lost much but the way it is they lost a lot of good muels and waggons. The Rebles are reported to be in forse there. I dont know whether we will go up there or not. It was the intention for us to go to Parkersburg when we came here and I dont know where we will go now.

Well, Jo, we herd some good news the other day but it turned out to be a hoax. The news was that fighting Jo had taken Richmond. The news are in our favor and I hope that they will take it yet.

We haint had much mail here since we left. I havent had a letter from home for a long time. I am anxious to here from home and how things are gowing on there. I told you when I got some place when I could I would write you the right kind of letter. I shant call this that one for this is as mean a place to write as ever I Saw. I cant write much at best and to take it on my knee I cant do anything. I want you to write soon and give me the news at home. I can not write much this time all that I can tell is that we are at Gauley Bridge and dont know where we will go next. So I will close for this time - give my love to all. Write soon I still remain yours as ever.

Will Leatherwood

I am out of stamps.

15 Jun 1863 - Gauley Bridge

Dear Brother

This extremely hot day I take my pen to let you know that I am well and dooing well. I have been looking for a letter from you for some time and thought I would get one today shure but it dident come. So I thought I would write one more to you. The weather is warm here. The days are hot and the nights are cool. It is a healthy place here the deauty is heavy. I go on picket evry fourth night. We are not allowed to have any fier or sleep any. It goes rite hard with me to keep awake all night but it dont go as hard now as it yoused to.

The news are tolearable good but not as good as I would like. Anything short of Vixburg dont soot me, I still think that Grant will take it but it is too long acoming. The Boys are all well pleased with the way they are deeling with traitors in Ohio. They haint hard enough for me if they had killed Vallandinghan and some more of his kind then it would pleas me.

Well Jo I hardly know how to write to you as there is nothing to write. You know more about how things are gowing on than I do. I dont know what to think of war, some of the Boys think it wont last long but I think it wont stop soon. We haint bothered much here with Rebs the reason is they are ordered other places. It will come our turn some day they say. They are gowing to make us get this fall they will have a good time of it I recon. Some of them Rebs at home think there is an abolition war now since the niggers are helping to put the Rebellion down. It is just the thing for me.

Well it must close some time and I dont care how soon. It is just ten months to day since we went into camp and I am better satisfied than I was then. I dont think as much about home. The Boys all treat me well and Gauley is my home.

I want you to write and tell me how things are gowing at home. I expect you are buisy now but it wont take you long some Sunday to write a few lines. Jo I would like to be there and help you to harvest but it would go hard with Me to work now I have got so ...

(bottom part of page torn off here)

that I am still alive I never had better health in my life. I am gowing to send two dollars in this and tell Em to buy Tammy and Willy something to remember me by. I would have sent some home but we only got two months pay and I thought it wouldent pay you to go after it but I must close for this time. Write soon as you can. Give my respects to all the friends and especily to the family, yours truly.

W. H. Leatherwood to his beloved Brother Joseph

29 June 1863 - Gauley Bridge, W.Va.[11]

Dear Brother

This hot day I once more attempt to rite you a few lines to let you know that I am still alive and well. Things are about as usual only our men had a little fight with the rebs the other day at Loop Creek.

There was twenty four men out of the four Companies that are here sent under command of Lt. Crofford to guard the wharf boat, six out of Co. E. The distance from here is six miles. They thought they would make a dash in there. There was two Cos. of the second Va. Cavelry sent from Piat to meet them. They did come but when they got up there instead of putting out pickets they all laid down and went to sleep and the Rebs come on them surprised and would have captured all of them if it hadent been for our Boys. But Lieutenant Crofford orderd them to fier which they done with a good effect. They hoisted five out of there saddles. Our Cavelry broke and run they all escaped but thirty five. They wer captured all ther hores and most of ther arms none of our Boys wer hurt. The firing was done across the River. That is the way they do it up here, they watch untill they get a chance at some weak place and then make a dash. But if our men had kept a good lookout they would have made them sorry for that but so it goes.

Well the next thing is some else the Pay master has been here for instance and give us our rations of greenbacks. We was paid for two months and I sent some more home. The pay agent dident come this time to take our money home. We all sent it to Galliapoliss and there check to West Union. Pap can draw it at the Bank. It haint as nice a way as we sent before but it was the best we could do. I sent thirty three dollars go as soon as you can and get it.

I received two letters from you last week but thought I wouldent write untill I know how the money would go. One of your letters was almost out of date it was rote on the 23rd of May some of them a long time a coming. I recon them Rebles are cutting a big dash down ther. Well evry dog has his day there time will come some of these days to go up and they will go up too mind if they dont. There will be some more after a while to do like Ean did that was good.

Jo you said you had a notion to enlist just take a fools advice and stay at home as long as you can. The war has only comenced and when I get home I will relieve you and then you can go. The news from the East is not verry good there haint much from below. Jo the way soldiers have to do up here _____ nerry plesant. I go on picket evry fore or five days and some times oftener set up all night and not sleep a wink. As far as the deauty is concerned I would rather be in front of Vixburg. The privates go on evry other day. The bush whackers ar getting thick here again. They are the devlishest set of men in the world. It is dangerous on picket but we have got so we dont mind it much.

Well Jo as I have no paper that is fit to rite on and not much to rite about I will have to close and rite again. Rite to me and let me know whether you get the money. If I was at home I could tell you a heap but I am here and expect to stay till the war is over or till my three years are up at any rate. I have just received a letter from America. I was sorry to here that Cate is sick. I hope she will get well soon.

---

[11] **Transcriber's note**: West Virginia had separated from Virginia and re-admitted to the Union as a separate state on June 20, 1863

I would rite more but the paper is so bad that I cant rite. It is a helthy a place here as I could get to. Mind that money will be sent to the bank you will have to receipt for it. I would have sent more but I bought a watch something that I couldent do without and kept a little. I believe that is all this time. Write bought a watch something that I couldent do without and kept a little. I believe that is all this time. Write as soon as you can give my love to Em and all the rest. Nothing more at present excuse my awkward way of writing, I am not advancing as fast in writing as I am in other things. If I live till this war is over it will be the best school that ever I went to. Good health and long life to you all Good bye.

W.H. Leatherwood

7 July 1863 - Gauley Bridge, W.Va.

Dear Brother

Yours of the 28th came to hand in due time and I was glad to here from home. The weather is still warm. There has ban rite smart of rain here at least I thought so yesterday and last night when on a picket post it rained for about two hours last night as hard as ever I saw it. I was on the hill just above camp in an open field. I had to stand and take it. There is no such thing as running to shelter her. If it hadent been for my gun blanket I would almost have drowned but as it was I didnt get much wet but for all it was verry disagreeable.

The news are good if what we here in true.[12] It is glorious both East and South. I was afeard that it is to good to be true but I will wait the truth of it. It done me good to here how the Boys stick up to the Butternuts. It would have done me good to have heard that they had killed old Ned if I had been there with my Springfield I could have shot him with as good grace as I could a Reble up here. I do hope the Boys wont let them go on as they have been dooing. I am glad to here that the Boys are still showing a willing mind by enlisting and helping us clean the Confederacy out. I still believe we will do it but dont know how long it will take us.

You spoke of the Boys wanting you to go. Now Jo I dont want you to go if you can help it. I dont see how they could get along at home without you and if they could it wont suit you. It goes hard with me to stay away from home a year and if you was to go and leave your little children you would want to see them more than once before you would get to. But if you do, dont go in the Infantry it is the hardest service there is. Go in with the 117th if you must go that is gowing to be a good birth for the boys. I wish I was there. I would like to have you with we verry much but it wont suit you as well here as there. They wont have to stand guard like we do dont go as long an you can help it. I wont say any thing about when the war will be over I have my own opinion about it.

I got booth of your letters. They was one a long time a coming. I got Enoses letter but dident answer rite away and got word that he was gon and did not know how to direct to him [9].[13] Give me his address. I let some of the Boys read your letter they say that brother of mine is rite in the head.

Well Jo I would rite you a long letter if there was any thing to rite about. I should like to see you all verry well. I must close soon I will have to send this without a stamp as I am just out. Write again soon, my health is good, I believe that is all this time give my love to all No more but remain your true friend and brother.

W.H. Leatherwood

---

[12]   **Transcriber's note**: The good news was Vicksburg and Gettysburg, both July 4th.
[13]   **Transcriber's note**: Enos Newlon, son of Tamzen (Nichols) Newlon, Emily's sister, who lived in the home neighborhood. (Name is sometimes spelled Newland.)

14 August 1863 - Fayetteville, Va.

TRANSCRIBER'S NOTES: *In the next letter Will teases Joe about Morgan's visit to southern Ohio. On July 4, 1963, not aware that Gettysburg and Vicksburg were lost, General Morgan crossed the Ohio into eastern Indiana, met some resistance, but turned east and swept across southern Ohio in what was chiefly a nuisance raid, taking food and horses as he went. At the Leatherwood farm some of his men took "Trim," the favorite saddle horse, frightened the girls and made them angry by taking "Pap" (aged 56) as well as Joseph some distance down the road at an uncomfortable pace. Tammy and Willy half remembered the incident, but their aunts never tired of telling the story to them and later to their younger brothers and sister. Morgan was captured in southeastern Ohio, and as Will mentions, some of the Union troops in West Virginia were sent to take care of the stragglers.*

General John Hunt Morgan's Raid across Indiana and Ohio, summer of 1864.

Dear Brother

Your letter came to hand in due time but as I had just rote to Kate I thought I would not answer for a few days and as this just makes me one year in the Service of Uncle Sam I thought I would write you a few lines.

I am well. The wether is warm and we are drilling some and fortyfying. In a week or too this place will be hard to get at. The Rebs will have some fun before they get it. They haint bothering us as much as they did. Colonel White is in command here. He is a bulley old fellow. He can talk with a private as well as an officer.

Well Jo I recon you dont want to soldier any more when old Morgan is in command. He drills new recruits rather hard. I shouldent like to be under him myself. He did play hob generaly but he is done now for a while. I couldent help laughing when I heard how they got you drawn in. I can imagine how you felt when they made you give up your gun but that was nothing. If they had only left Trim you run a resk and a grait one to follow them. If they had got you again you would have went up the spout. I am Sorry that I dident get to see some of you that followed up but there was a poor chance to get to see any one. We was on the move all the time when we was at Buffington. I heard that the Seventh Ohio Cavelry was up the River a mile or too. I started to go up but when I got pretty near there they had gon on a scout. We was only there about four hours. I would have liked to have saw the Boys the best in the world but a soldier cant have his way in such things.

It may be that we will get to see each other some time. I have an idea we will stay here all winter again. If we do and I dont get to come home I want you to come up here. There haint been much news

here for a few days the last was Taviarable from Charleston. It is here just like it used to be at home, they all say now when we get a certain place then the war will be over and as soon as we get it then there is an other. My opinion is it wont stop...

(bottom part of page torn off)

...if it is so pretty I want to see it. Give my love to all, nothing more but remain yours as ever.

W. H. Leatherwood

25 September 1863 - Fayetteville, W.Va.

Dear Brother,

After a delay of some days I will try to write you a few lines. Your letter came to hand in due time but we was under order to go on out post duty for ten days and I had no time to answer before we went and dident take any paper to write on. So I had to wait untill I came back. I am well it is raining some today. The Boys are all in good spirits, the news are not so good as they have been. The report is that Old Rosey has got a thrashing I am afraid it is true.

Jo I am sorry to here that the people are gowing so mad in political matters, it is the worst thing for us that could be we are all or nearly all a unit for Brough. There are some in the Regiment that will vote for Vallandingham but I dont think that there is one in our Company. The Val men are few and far between. I am astonished to see free Americans act so.

I showed your letter to some of the boys and it pleased them well. One of them red it and then asked me if he mite read it to the mess. I toled him he mite. He red it and the Boys all said you was all rite.

I was sorry to here that you was not stout but it is a consolation to know that you are where you can take care of your self.

Well Jo I think that you had better make one trip up to W.Va. This winter it will pay you to come I want you to go to Old Sam Teener and get him to make me a good pare of boots for this winter and if you can come I would like for you to bring them up also my over coat and a vest. I am not certain whether I can come home this winter or not. I wont need them things for a month or more but have them made rite away.

I have been looking for a letter from home for a few days now and when I here how Leah is I will know more about it. I can get a ten day furlow after a while but I couldent more than go and come in that time. If she gets better I will not come for a while. If I dont come I would like for you or Pap one to come up and see me. It shant cost you nothing to come only your time. There is nothing of interest gowing on here. So I will close for the present. I will tell you what I will do in my next. If you cant come I will let you know how you can send them, nothing more will write soon yours truly.

W.H. Leatherwood

1 October 1863 - Fayetteville, W.Va.

Dear Brother,

Your letter was received and read with grait interest. It found me in the best of health and tolerable spirits. The news we here is considerable mixed up, there haint much information to be got from them.

There seems to be more Politics than any thing else. The people must be gowing wild. They act as though there was nothing else gowing on. They dont think of the war any more at least it dont look so to me. Instead of trying to put it down they are trying to make more, if they had to play soldier a while they would forget their politicks. I tell you there hant much quarling among the soldiers they are about all of the same opinion.

The Pay master has made us another visit and give us two months pay. I am gowing to send some money home this time. The pay agent was here this time and caried our money home for us. I am gowing to send my receipt in this and you can get the money at West Union. It is the best and safest way to send it. Our clothing bill was settled this time.

I am sending thirty dollars. If you get me a pair of boots pay for them out of it and if you get in the notion of comming up take what will pay your way. I shall not try to come home for a while. Well I believe I have written all that is nessary. All the news we get is in the papers and you get them before we do.

We have the forts all done. The probability is that we will stay here this winter. There is something gowing on here. You must write as often as you can. The Boys, when I get a letter, want to know if it is from my brother and if it is they want to read it. Tell Willey he must not grow so big that Uncle Will wont know him. I would give one months wages to see him and Tammy. Give my love to all the family nothing more at this time yours as ever.

Will Leatherwood

26 October 1863 - Fayetteville, W.Va.

Dear Brother,

Well Joseph, this morning I will write you a few lines to inform you that I am well. Your letter was received and read with grait interest. I am truely glad your dream did not turn out as you thought it would. I never had better health than I have had this fall but it may not last long.

The election went off all rite. Here the Adams County boys done the clean thing for Brough but there was some traitors in this Regiment. There was seven in the 91st shame on such beastly ignorant things in the shape of men. I here that the citizens elected the Union ticket. I say bully for Old Adams. The Boys are all well pleased with the result.

We are working on our winter quarters have them about half done. It has been the talk for some time that we will go away but I hardly think we will. If we go any where it will be out to Louisburg to clean them out of there that is sixty miles from here. If we go we will come back here to winter. There is a Company out of the Briggade out scouting. They destroyed a large amount of property for the rebs at the Sulpher Springs the other day.

I am sorry you did not get my Boots in that box but if you cant send them I can get along without them. We are having a meeting here now. There was preaching last night. It makes me think of home to here a Sermon.

I was sorry to here of them Brave Boys loosing there lives down there in the late battle that was a grait Slaughter. I got a letter from Frank Messinger he was in front nearly all the time he said Stone River was nowhere to it.

Well Jo I have allmost give up the idea of this war closing any ways soon at least during my term of enlistment and dont know as I shall ever get home or not. They are slow giving furlows I believe I have told you all I can think of now. I cant write much at a time without telling one thing over so often.

I cant tell how well I would love to see all of you. I would like for you to come up but if you cant get time dont come. I am gowing to send you a kind of a report of the way the election went a full report of the two Adams Co. Companies. You will see the 91st has the most traitors in the Brigade four of them from Sciote County Co. C.

But I must close for this time, write soon, give my love to all the family yours as ever.

Will Leatherwood

P.S. Since writing there has a furlow come for Billy Moore. He lives in West Union he has got a sick furlow he will stay twenty days or he has a furlow for that time and I will send this by him with an other ... I have it, wont do me any good here it may be of sole use some day thats all.

27 December 1863 - Fayetteville, West Va,

Dear Brother,

Your welcome sheets was received on last evening and was read with grait interest. I must tell you what I was doing. I was seated on my bunk watching the Boys roast a big gobler. We had a rite time over him. The weather is bad it is raining to day this has been a dry Christmas to me some of the boys got whiskey and had a drunk but that was no fun to me.

We have just herd what our last raid on Lewisburg was for. It was to draw the attention of the Rebs while General Averill cut the railroad he has done it all right and got out safe. Well I should love to see them trembling sinners. Their time is almost up. They will soon know what there doom is. If it only takes the rite ones then I will be satisfied. But it is as like to take good men as them traitors. The news are good so far as I have heard some of the Boys are fanc(y) ing the war will close next summer but I cant see it. In that light I hope it will, for if there was ever a boy sick of any thing, it is me of this cruel war. There is still talk of us gowing down on the River. I would rather stay here as we have the best quarters in the Valley but they just say go and we go. The Soldiers life is rather a hard one some times. I get discouraged and dont care for any thing and then I get over that but dont get in the notion of dooing like them lads in tha artilery. That is just what I expected of such Soldiers if I herd the truth and I think I did that was that they voted for Vallandingham, couldent expect any thing better.

I was glad to here that you had got your crib done. I would love to come home and see you all this winter but I cant tell whether I will or not. They are giving some furlows but the married men go first and that is rite. I would not ask for one untill they go. Well Jo I cant think or any thing to write about and will close. My head is verry foggy today, tell Kate that I wil write to her soon give my love to all. I still remain yours as ever.

Will Leatherwood

19 January 1864 - Fayetteville, W.Va.

Dear Brother Jo,

Your letter bearing date of the ninth was received last evening although it was short it was read with much interest, long letters are not always the best. The weather is cold today our Company just came off of three days picket. Last evening the weather was rather pleasant while we were out but since we came in it has frozen up and now it is snowing.

You spoke of the cold weather and wanted to know how I got along. It has been verry cold here since new year at least part of the time. I was on deauty Sunday after new year but did not suffer any from the cold. I can stand more than I use to and have plenty of clothes. Uncle Sam clothes us well if we dont get much else all I have suffered this winter was when we went to Lewisburg. I did suffer then it rained so such and was so cold we had to wade several creeks.

There is no news here of importance to write more than you get in the papers. The Boys are all well. You have the start of me, you can write about the weddings that are gowing off. There is nothing of that find goes off up here. I am glad they are still willing to make soldiers if they wont come and be Soldiers them selves but there are butternuts enough now. If I mistake not there will be a surprise party before a year rolles around that will surprise them more than they are looking for. If this thing haint closed before the next Presidential Campaign there will be fun rather dier fun though at least that is my opinion of the matter. I hope old Butler wil get a chance to try his hand on Richmond. It wil be a grand thing if he has luck.

Well Jo as I have to get some wood I will close I am well and harty. Give my love to all the family. I would love to see Em and the Children, write when ever you can, nothing more still remain yours as ever.

Will Leatherwood

11 February 1864 - Fayetteville, W.Va.

Dear Jo,

As I have some spare time I wil write you a few lines to let you know how I am getting along. I am well. I received your letter on the eighth but could not answer then on the morning of the tenth went on picket but now I am at your service and wil give you a few items. Whether they wil be of any interest to you I wil leave for you to decide. There is nothing of any grait interest gowing on here.

We had some little excitement the other day about old Granny Scammon. He was captured at red house on the third. There wer but few teers shed in this Brigade. I hope he will have a good time of it.

Wel I told you that I was on Picket and while I was out, there was six rebs come in and gave themselves up. I was on the out post so I just sent them to head quarters under guard. They had hardly got out of sight until there wer three of our Boys come in. They had been captured at Chikkamauga and taken to Danville where they broke guard. They had worked there way thrue safe. Poor fellows they sufferd a graideel. They had traveled twenty three nights in the cold. They came laughing. There has a good many come in this way. There is no end to the rebs they come in nearly every day. They report the Confederacy gon up, hope it is so. They are conscripting every thing in this State they can get. I suppose them fellows think they are safe if they had known that Old Abe was gowing to make another Reckuisition on them, they would have stayed away longer.

If any of them ladies comes around with there subscription just tell them to put me down on it and I wil pay when I get home. I would to be there to see the Boys that have reenlisted, I rather think they wil have a hi old time. But three years is a big contract for to get thirty days furlow the opinion of most of the Boys is that the war wont last long. I hope they are rite but I cant see it that way.

We were paid off the other day but there is no way to send the money home I have thirty dollars I wish you had. The pay agent did not come this time. I believe I have written all that is nessary for this time. Write when ever you can. It dont matter to me if they are rong side up I can read them. Give my love to Em and the Babies, nothing more, Stil remain your afectionate brother

Will

28 February 1864 - Fayetteville, W.Va.[14]

Well Jo,

Yours of the eighteenth is before me and I hasten to reply it found me in good helth. I was glad to here from home and here that you and the rest wer all well. The River has been closed for some time so that we did not get any mail but it is open now. The weather has again opened and is pleasent. We had some colder weather than we had the other cold spell.

There is but little gowing on here Old General Crook has command of this Division now. We may look for to do something the coming summer. Some think we wil make a forward move in the Spring but it is uncertain we may and we may not. Such a thing is that we may stay here all Summer although I dont promis my self any thing of the kind. A Soldier cant see his destiny two hours ahead he cant tell when he wil get orders to go or where he wil go.

I was glad to here that there wer some of the Boys gowing in yet but I would be like you stay and see the last cat hung. There are grait inducements for a man to go, one that loves money. I thought some of them you spoke of would be the last ones to go glad they have, they have got as good a rite as any one.

I would love to be at home to see the Boys that are on furlow. I did not know that Hi Easton was in the Service. How I heard he had resigned again. Wel I have but little to write. I would be glad to get home to see Tammy and Willey but have no hopes of it as long as I keepe well and all of the family it is of but little use for me to come home. It would be a grait pleasure to see all of you. You neede not look for me any way soon. Tell Em that I have a present for her which I wil send some of these days but I must close. Write soon yours truley.

Will Leatherwood

---

9 May 1864 - Cloyd's Mountain, West Virginia[15]

The article provides an excellent summary of the action undertaken on 9 May 1864 at Cloyd's Mountain where William H. Leatherwood gave "...the last full measure of devotion that a soldier can lay upon his countries altar, his life." The article appeared originally in the *Raleigh Herald* as, "When the Long Roll Sounded In Gen Crook's Camp, Fayetteville, May 3, 1864," By Captain J. H. Prather, of the 91st Ohio.

May 3, 1864, marked a remarkable epoch in the history of the Civil War. The slogan had sounded the forward movement of the Army of the Potomac. The long roll had sounded in General Sherman's fortified camp at Chattanooga, Chickamauga, and Lookout Mountain. The union forces were in motion west of the Mississippi. General Siegel [sic: Sigel] had ordered the forward movement of the federal army in the Shenandoah Valley and General Crook, the noted Indian fighter headed 7,000 trained and seasoned soldiers for a raid on Cloyd's Mountain, Dublin Depot and New River Bridge and the destruction of the Virginia and Tennessee R.R. It was deemed of vital importance to wreck the roads and destroy the bridge over the New River and thus permanently crippling their line of communication between Richmond, Virginia, and northern Georgia.

General Grant had about 114,000 veterans under his immediate command to assail General Lee's Confederate Army of 100,000 soldiers in the Wilderness, Spotsylvania and South Anna. His trusted time tried and fire tested General William T. Sherman with his 100,000 splendidly equipped and magnificent army, moved across the mountains of northern Georgia, and at Kenesaw, Resaca, Dalton and Lost Mountain the thunder of his canon and the roll of musketry could be heard every day for more than a month until his victorious battalions appeared at the Gate City of the south and there laid tribute to its immense spoil despoiled it of its arsenal and munition of was, humbled its pride into the dust, applied to the torch to the city and depopulated it of its inhabitants. And when the mayor of the city made a plea for him to rescind his order, the General said: "War is hell and you cannot define it. My plans are such that I cannot fairly discuss them with you, but they make it necessary for men, women and children to leave the city and I will cheerfully facilitate that egress. But when this cruel war is ended, come to me and I will gladly share with your people my last cracker." Magnanimous words from a great military leader.

The long rolls sounded throughout General Crook's camp at Fayetteville, West Virginia on the morning of May 3, 1864 and was greeted by thunderous applause from the throats of 7,000 Union soldiers and perhaps in a little less than an hour the column was in motion headed for south West Virginia via Raleigh, Flat Top Mountain, Princeton and Shannon's Crossroads. [Note: Shannon's Crossroads is located near Princeton, West Virginia.]

There was a big fort at Princeton with General Breckenridge blazoned and greenswards across its front and which the Yankees cut a bit and substituted Fort Crook. At Shannon's Crossroads and attempt was made to intercept two Confederate regiments that were marching to the aid of the Confederate entrenchments at Cloyd's Mountain only 6 miles away.

---

[15]   The following article is from the *Raleigh Herald*, Beckley, WV, 29 April 1909, and was transcribed by Darrell Helton. The article appeared as "91st Ohio at Cloyd's Mountain WV," by Darrell Helton, *Ohio Civil War Genealogy Journal*, Volume XVI, Issue 4 (# 64), 2012, page 221-222. The article is copyright © Ohio Genealogical Society, Ohio Civil War Genealogy Society, 2012.

The march 24 miles made this day was very fatiguing and the advanced guard of the Union forces only reached this point in time to skirmish with the rear guard of the Confederate regiments which had just passed by. We were now about 100 miles from Fayette and in the immediate presence of a well-armed, entrenched and defiant force under General Jenkins. A telegraph instrument was seized and it being discovered that the line had not been severed, the Union operator called up to know of the rebel operator, "How many rebels at Cloyd's Mountain?" and promptly came back the answer, "Enough to whip all the Yankees at Shannon's Crossroads."

It was evident, at this point, where we had bivouacked for the night that Captain S. E. Clark commanding our company E had a premonition or presentment, that only morrow he would be called to pay the last full measure of devotion that a soldier can lay upon his countries altar, his life. As the sun sank to rest beyond the western horizon he said: "I will never see another sun go down." And when the drums sounded taps he said, "Boys let us lie down and take a rest for we will never all again bivouac together in this life."

On the morning of May 9 at 4 AM the advanced guard of General Crook's army moved out on the Cloyd's Mountain road followed at once by the entire force and the skirmishing, at once, became sharp, continuous and heavy. The rebel leader, General Jenkins, was very confident that with his 5000 entrenched Johnnies, he could inflict a crushing defeat on the Union force that was sent to dislodge them. So confident was he of that he brought out to the battlefield a number of ladies from Dublin Depot to witness the fight and arrayed in some prophet's mantle said, "I will whip the Yankees today or I will never fight again." And never did prophetical prediction meet with swifter fulfillment than this as that was the last battle General Jenkins ever fought.

The rebel pickets stubbornly contested the ground, sheltering themselves behind trees and stumps, yielding gradually until they were pushed back onto the main body within the entrenchments. The 2nd Brigade of which the 91st Ohio formed a part fled up a ravine that debauched slightly from the main road in order to flank the rebel skirmishers and then began the ascent of a steep and lofty mountain and on reaching the summit, a magnificent and … unfolded itself to the vision. There on the opposing mountain were the rebel entrenchments with the long serpent like lines moving into position assigned them. Back of it all was the broad and undulating table land with its diversified memory. In the valley before us was considerable overconfidence of thrift and culture. The browsing cattle and sheep, the substantial and neat farm houses, the meadows and woodland. Out in front of the Confederate rifle ports is an apple orchard where a brass cannon beautifully, reflecting the rays of the morning sun and firing at the head of the Federal column and as the conflict became closer and sharper it was drawn back into the enemies works.

It now became evident that our brigade was to be employed as a flaking column and passing far around to the enemies right through a long and narrow ravine. About 10 o'clock the head of a column came in sight of an epaulment redoubt behind which there were Johnnies in abundance and two or more cannon. The ground here was very unfavorable for a good alignment and a quick development but the two advance regiments filed into position as rapidly as possible with the Virginia Union and the 91st Ohio going into position on quick time. The Rebels in their works were quick to take advantage of the hasty formation and came over their entrenchments tumultuously cheering and firing as they charged.

The roll of musketry now became tremendous and deafening all along the line inasmuch it drowned the reports of the cannon. The two advance regiments were at once thrown into panic, confusion and rout and passed through our ranks like a flock of frightened sheep. They were the same who had called us "Forty dollar conscripts" and said "We would run to a man the first stiff fight we would get into." Col. Turley was adept at profanity and exhausted his vocabulary of cuss words and told them "to get out of the way and let men go in."

Then came the order to throw off knapsack and get ready to charge. A Bible which my mother had presented me was in my knapsack and I ran hastily to the rear and secured it and heard some of my comrades shouting coward but I quickly returned to my position in the ranks. Across the back of my flyleaf she had inscribed the 1st Psalm. "Blessed is the man that walketh not in the counsel of the ungodly, nor standeth in the way of sinners nor sitteth in the seat of the scornful. But his delight is in the law of the Lord and in his law doth he meditate day and night. And he shall … not wither and whatsoever he doeth shall prosper. The ungodly are not so: but are like the chaff which the wind driveth away. Therefore the ungodly shall not stand in the judgement, nor the sinners in the congregation of the righteous. For the Lord knoweth the way of righteous: But the way of the ungodly shall perish." A real gem of inspiration.

OCWGS Editor's Notes: for further information on General Crook's operation to cut the Virginia and Tennessee Railroad at Dublin Junction in May 1864, see *91st Ohio Volunteer Infantry with the Civil War Letters of Lieutenant Colonel Benjamin Franklin Coates*, Lois J. Lambert, Milford, Oh: Little Miami Publishing Company, 2005, page 35-37. A map of the expedition is included with Colonel Coates' description of the operation, written on 19 May 1864. The Virginia and Tennessee Railroad was cut at Dublin Depot, severing communications between the Confederate armies of Joseph Johnston in Georgia and Robert E. Lee in Virginia. Captain Samuel E. Clark and Corporal William H. Leatherwood were killed in the fighting on 9 May 1864 at Cloyd's Mountain; Private John H. Gillen died the following day of his wound; Corporal Thomas Hughes was wounded, captured and died as a prisoner of war; and five men were captured and survived their imprisonment at Andersonville, Georgia.

Confederate Brigadier General Albert Gallatin Jenkins, a Harvard Law School graduate and lawyer in Charleston, West Virginia was wounded and captured on 9 May at Cloyd's Mountain. Unable to recover from the wound and the amputation of his arm at the shoulder, he died on 21 May 1864 (Warner, *Generals in Gray*, 154-155).

Part II

The Civil War Letters of Joseph D. Leatherwood to his wife Emily Leatherwood

A Pedigree Chart for
Joseph D. Leatherwood

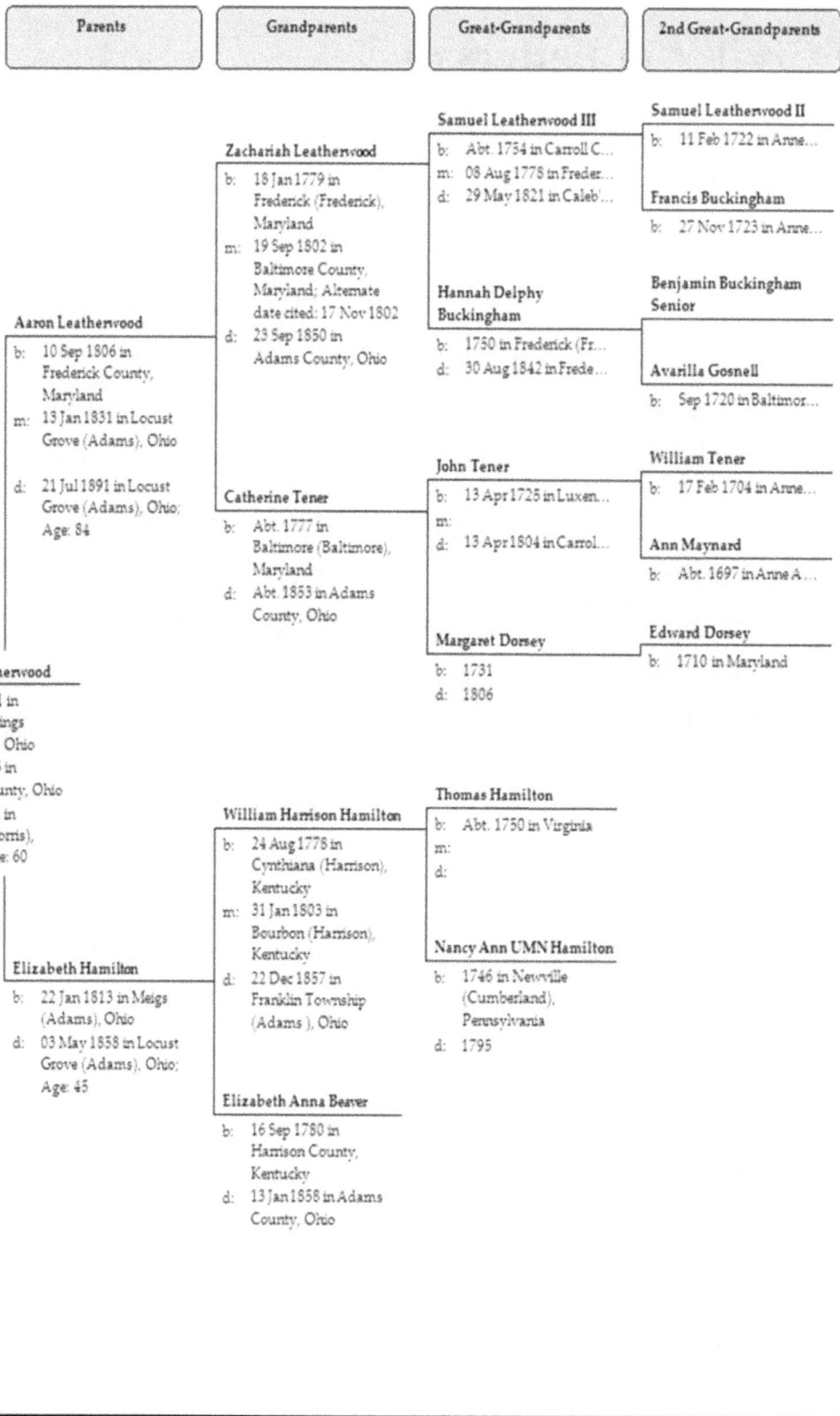

Parents	Grandparents	Great-Grandparents	2nd Great-Grandparents

Zachariah Leatherwood
b: 18 Jan 1779 in Frederick (Frederick), Maryland
m: 19 Sep 1802 in Baltimore County, Maryland; Alternate date cited: 17 Nov 1802
d: 23 Sep 1850 in Adams County, Ohio

Samuel Leatherwood III
b: Abt. 1754 in Carroll C...
m: 08 Aug 1778 in Freder...
d: 29 May 1821 in Caleb'...

Samuel Leatherwood II
b: 11 Feb 1722 in Anne...

Francis Buckingham
b: 27 Nov 1723 in Anne...

Hannah Delphy Buckingham
b: 1750 in Frederick (Fr...
d: 30 Aug 1842 in Frede...

Benjamin Buckingham Senior

Avarilla Gosnell
b: Sep 1720 in Baltimor...

Aaron Leatherwood
b: 10 Sep 1806 in Frederick County, Maryland
m: 13 Jan 1831 in Locust Grove (Adams), Ohio
d: 21 Jul 1891 in Locust Grove (Adams), Ohio; Age: 84

Catherine Tener
b: Abt. 1777 in Baltimore (Baltimore), Maryland
d: Abt. 1853 in Adams County, Ohio

John Tener
b: 13 Apr 1725 in Luxen...
m:
d: 13 Apr 1804 in Carrol...

William Tener
b: 17 Feb 1704 in Anne...

Ann Maynard
b: Abt. 1697 in Anne A...

Margaret Dorsey
b: 1731
d: 1806

Edward Dorsey
b: 1710 in Maryland

Joseph D. Leatherwood
b: 23 Dec 1831 in Sinking Springs (Highland), Ohio
m: 09 Oct 1856 in Adams County, Ohio
d: 02 Jun 1892 in Dunlap (Morris), Kansas; Age: 60

William Harrison Hamilton
b: 24 Aug 1778 in Cynthiana (Harrison), Kentucky
m: 31 Jan 1803 in Bourbon (Harrison), Kentucky
d: 22 Dec 1857 in Franklin Township (Adams), Ohio

Thomas Hamilton
b: Abt. 1750 in Virginia
m:
d:

Nancy Ann UMN Hamilton
b: 1746 in Newville (Cumberland), Pennsylvania
d: 1795

Elizabeth Hamilton
b: 22 Jan 1813 in Meigs (Adams), Ohio
d: 03 May 1858 in Locust Grove (Adams), Ohio; Age: 45

Elizabeth Anna Beaver
b: 16 Sep 1780 in Harrison County, Kentucky
d: 13 Jan 1858 in Adams County, Ohio

Family Group Sheet for Joseph D. Leatherwood

Husband:	Joseph D. Leatherwood	
Birth:	23 Dec 1831 in Sinking Springs (Highland), Ohio	
Marriage:	09 Oct 1856 in Adams County, Ohio	
Death:	02 Jun 1892 in Dunlap (Morris), Kansas; Age: 60	
Burial:	Aft. 02 Jun 1892 in Dunlap (Morris), Kansas	
Father:	Aaron Leatherwood	
Mother:	Elizabeth Hamilton	

Wife:	Emily Pleasant Nichols	
Birth:	13 Jan 1833 in Loudoun County, Virginia	
Burial:	1882 in Dunlap (Morris), Kansas	
Death:	13 Sep 1882 in Dunlap (Morris), Kansas	
Father:	Enos Ennis West Nichols	
Mother:	Edna Hoge Gregg	

Children:

1 F	Name:	Tamzen Jane "Tammie" Leatherwood
	Birth:	01 Feb 1858 in Sinking Springs (Highland), Ohio
	Marriage:	04 Jun 1891 in Dunlap (Morris), Kansas
	Burial:	Mar 1933 in Salina (Saline), Kansas; Buried: Roselawn Memorial Cemetery
	Death:	26 Mar 1933 in Salina (Saline), Kansas; Age: 75
	Spouse:	Francis William Fenn

2 M	Name:	William R. "Willy" Leatherwood
	Birth:	07 Jun 1859 in Sinking Springs (Highland), Ohio
	Marriage:	21 Dec 1882 in Dunlap (Morris), Kansas
	Death:	28 Jan 1935 in Burlington (Skagit), Washington; Age: 76
	Burial:	30 Jan 1935 in Burlington (Skagit), Washington
	Spouse:	America Elizabeth Ryman

3 F	Name:	Hannah Elizabeth Leatherwood
	Birth:	11 Feb 1861 in Sinking Springs (Highland), Ohio
	Death:	06 Mar 1862 in Sinking Spring (Highland), Ohio
	Burial:	08 Mar 1862 in Sinking Spring (Highland), Ohio

4 F	Name:	Anna M. Leatherwood
	Birth:	15 Dec 1862 in Sinking Springs (Highland), Ohio
	Death:	30 Mar 1887 in Ohio; Age: 24
	Burial:	02 Apr 1887 in Dunlap (Morris), Kansas
	Spouse:	Dennis Clark

5 M	Name:	Samuel Townsend Leatherwood
	Birth:	09 Sep 1866 in Sinking Springs (Highland), Ohio
	Marriage:	22 Feb 1894 in Panoia (Delta), Colorado
	Death:	23 Dec 1936 in Panoia (Delta), Colorado; Age: 70
	Burial:	24 Dec 1936 in Panoia (Delta), Colorado
	Spouse:	Susan Sarah Thomas

6	Name:	Macy Edwin Leatherwood	
M	Birth:	16 Sep 1869 in Sinking Springs (Highland), Ohio	
	Marriage:	12 Jul 1899 in Morris County, Kansas	
	Death:	19 Oct 1943 in Council Grove (Morris), Kansas; Age: 72	
	Burial:	21 Oct 1943 in Council Grove (Morris), Kansas	
	Spouse:	Nita Pearl Holcomb	

7	Name:	Roscoe Aaron Leatherwood	
M	Birth:	09 Feb 1872 in Sinking Springs (Highland), Ohio	
	Marriage:	20 Jul 1904 in Seattle (King), Washington	
	Death:	27 Feb 1935 in Elk River (Clearwater), Idaho; Age: 62	
	Burial:	01 Mar 1935 in Moscow (Latah), Idaho	
	Spouse:	Emma J. Jones	

8	Name:	Joseph Harlan Leatherwood	
M	Birth:	20 May 1874 in Sinking Springs (Highland), Ohio	
	Marriage:	26 Aug 1903 in Centralia (Lewis), Washington	
	Death:	28 Feb 1945 in Centralia (Lewis), Washington; Age: 70	
	Burial:	02 Mar 1945 in Centralia (Lewis), Washington	
	Spouse:	Edith May Price	

Notes:

Camp Cleveland, March the 22nd 1864[16]

Dear Pleasy,

After a stroll over the city and to the dock to look at the vessels and geting a look at General Tom Thumb and his wife, Commodore Nut and partner, and their minature carriage and ponies, I seat myself in my bunk with the boys all around me laughing and talking and singing, for to try to pen you a few lines to let you know that I am well and in good spirits.

I bunk with Denis and Danny, we are all here in quarters together and get a long very well. They are all rather civil no drinking at all in our shack there is some card playing that is all. I was out to look at the Lake. You can look away out on the water and it looks like a great blue mountain covered with snow.

It is said that we will leave here tomorrow but it is uncertain about that. I want you to tell Tam that the provision she gave me did me a great service. It kept me from suffering and I have some of it yet. It was a great favor to me for which I am very much obliged to her.

As I wrote to you once already and once to Will I shall not write a long leter. I hope this may find you all well and in good spirits, keep your heads up, recollect us at all times. Talk to the dear little children about pappy, tell Tammy and Willy that Pappy wants them to be good children and not forget him. I hope you got my letter and understood what was in it. The weather is cold. This is the first day that it has not snowed since we have ben here. If you want to write to me you can direct to Camp Cleveland and it will folow me.

I dont know of any thing more at present but remain your afectionate Companion til death, give my love to all of the friends.

Joseph to. Emily P. Leatherwood.

Direct to Mr. Joseph Leatherwood, Camp Cleveland Ohio. In care of Capt. Easton, Co. L, 2nd OVC, to folow regmt.

---

[16] **Transcriber's Note:** There are not many letters from Joseph Leatherwood himself, though many of his diary entries are about letters received from or written to Emily, his sisters, and his sister-in-law "Tam" Newlon. The letter on page 56, dated July 6, 1864, from Knoxville, Tenneessee, was written by Tam Newlon's son, Enos. It gives some indication of the close family-neighborhood feeling among the Ohio kinfolk. It is written to Emily P. Leatherwood.

Camp Stoneman, Head Quarters 2nd OVC
Sunday April the 24th, 1864

Dear Pleasy,

This beautiful day finds me seated on the hights over looking the town of Alexandria and the Potomac. It is one of the finest views I ever saw. The River dotted over with vessels of all kinds and the hills with camp's as far as I can see. If you could just stand by my side one moment you would see sights that would make your blood run cold, thousands of men camped ready to move to the deadly conflict, the long lines of wagons as far as the eye can reach. My heart sickens at the sight, war, war, everything wears a war like appearance. Near us is a large fort its huge guns frowning angrily out in every direction. O that the time may soon Come when there shall be no use for them.

We are here in the dismounted camp we struck tents on the 21st, marched to the Railroad, layed out in open field over night the 22nd, started for Washington City got there in the after noon, got out dinner at the soldiers home after which I went to the Capitol and went all over it or nearly so. It is one of the finest things in this world I wish you could see it. We stayed all night in the city and until after noon then started for this camp. We marched to the landing, got on boats, came acrost to a point 1.5 miles landed and marched to this place which is about 3 or 4 miles from the city.

We have not got any arms yet nor cant tell when we will. There are thousands of rumors in camp as to what will be done with us, some say we we will stay here for some time some say we will leave soon but none of them know. We will have to be armed and mounted before we take the field.

I received a letter from Tam last Monday the last letter that I have had. I wrote to the girls and thot to have got an answer before now but it has not come yet. I am well and harty, can eat anything that I can get, we have had plenty of soft bread and pork, beef and coffee but now it is hard tack instead of the soft bread.

I have been on Drill every day that there has been Drill since the 7th day of April. I was put at the head of the company and think that I may be the best looking soldier in the Company.

I put some rings in the leter to the girls and shal be sorry if they were miscarried they were for the children, poor little fellows how I would love to see them. Who that has not left a home and family can appreciate the comforts of one, how sweet the name of home sounds in the soldiers ear. I hope I shal live to enjoy the comforts of home.

When I started from the camp near Annapolis I gave my old coat to a poor old Negro and there has just come an order to camp for all who have citizens clothes to turn them in to the Goverment so I shal have to give up my pants. I cant send them home it wont pay, if there was any old Negro here I would give them to him.

Well her it is all still and nothing else still and quiet on the Potomac. I hope to hear from you soon you must try to write to me once a week, write about everything you can think of, commence Sunday and write every day till the letter is done.

Well Tamy and Willy, pappy is well and hopes his little children are well, it pleases pappy to hear that you think about him and talk about him, he wants you to be good children mind what mother says to you you suit not be saucy to Grandpap and the girls you must go to school and learn to read and write so you can rite to pap. You must not fight nor quarrel but be pretty children take good care of Puss and Jack and old Bird til pappy comes home. I must close my letter for the present.

Joseph Leatherwood to his Companion E.P. Leatherwood & Children

Direct to Washington D.C. Care of Capt. Easton Co. L, 2nd Reg. OVC, To Follow Regmt.

6 July 1864 - Knoxville, Tenn.

Dear Aunt,

I take my seat this morning to let you know that I have not forgotten you yet all tho I have not wrote to you since I left home. This leaves me well and I hope it my find you all enjoying the same blessings. I enjoy my self very well heare as well as I did at Covington if not better. We are campt near Fort Sanders east of Knoxville rite in the hot sun not a shade tree in the camp. There is an orcherd clost that we tend very regular about now to find a cool place to sleep.

For some two or three days now we have bin live very hi and at the top of the pot we have been picking blackberries and stewing some and haveing some baked in to pies. An old Negrow woman dose our bakeing and dose it very cheap. We had four pies for supper last night and have got enough berries to make as many more.

I want you to write to me and tell me how to direct a letter to uncle Joseph and how he is geting a long since he left Washington. I was sorry to heare of William being killed it made me think of days that are passed, of the many young men that I ust to love to be with that have died and bin killed since this infernal war broke out. I believe that I am the only one left of boys that ust to meet at Mr. Leatherwoods with his two boys and have such good times.

I havent told you about the health of the company. A.R. Fulton, S. Conaulay, O. Garman are all well and the Co. in general hac good health. We have plenty to eat such as it is. We dont get any beans nor hominy but get good meat, coffee, shugar and crackers and soft bread. Go on guard three times a week and drill two hours a day.

Well I must close you must excuse all mistakes and bad writing. write soon,

Yours respectfully E.U. Newlon[17]

---

[17] **Transcriber's note**: Tam Newlon's son.

6 February 1865 - Camp Russell, VA.

Dear Wife,

I take the present oportunity to inform you that I am in pretty good health and hope this may find you enjoying the same blessing. It seems to me a long time since I heard from any of you and I am geting impatient for to get some news. There is but little to break the monotony of camp life save the rumors of peace that come to us. Some put great confidence in them and even dare to say that there will be no campaign opened this spring but I cant think so, they will fight.

Some of our men came in this morning from a scout to Mofield[18] they ran into a rebel conscription camp and captured some prisoners. Scouting, picketing, and grand reviews are about all that we have to go through. I just came off picket today and thot that I would drop you a few lines, it was very cold and I could hardly keep from freezing. Well here comes Sergeant Campbell with a letter and I must stop and read.

It is Jan. 29. Well I am glad to hear that you are all well but sorry you are so disapointed about me coming home. You need not be afraid to fasten the door. I hope to get home but fear that it will be a long time first. I think that Harry was a fool to tell such stories at home as he did you must not be mutch disapointed if I dont come.

I am thinking of being transfered to Infantry Service thinking that it is about as good as the Cavalry if I can get to a Reg. of my choice think that I shal go. You can still send on your letters dont wait for a furlo, thinking that I wont get them.

You said that you was afraid the Rebels had got me, they wont get me if I have a horse of any accent without getting some of the rest. I have learnt to look out for myself pretty well. Tell Billy that pappy had a harty laugh for his slay rid,but think he had better not ride with the oxen any moire. I wish that I was at home to take him a sleigh ride.

It is snowing here today the 7th it looks as if there was going to be quite a snow, things are dull here now, no pay yet nor no prospect for any tor some time to Cole. I al out of writtag paper and stamps and if you dont get letters often, dont be unesy for be sure that I am all right. I wrote to Adlaid some time ago if you see her ask her if she got the letter. I have got some that I have not answered nor cant for som time. Tell me what has become of Sarah she has not sent me that letter she told you she would. As there is nothing of interest here I will close hoping to hear from some of you soon. I as yours till death. Joseph to Emily P. Leatherwood

---

[18] **Transcriber's note**: Mofield, probably Moorefield, W Va., some distance west of the Shenandoah Valley where the regiment was located.

24 March 1865 - Whitehouse Landing, VA.

Dear Wife,

I take the present oportunity to drop you a few lines to let you know that I am still alive and well and hope this may find you the same. I received the letters from you, one from Tam, [and] one each from Sod and Town yesterday evening when I come off picket. I was truly glad to hear from you that you was all well.[19]

As I before stated to you we landed here on the 18th and are still here after a march of near five hundred miles through rain, mud and fording and swimming deep and rapid rivers drowning men and horses but through the mercy and providence of God I am safe and sound.

I made some incorrece statements in my last [letter] as to the distance from here to the James River. I was in a hurry and took flying reports for truth so you will have to sift my letters. There are many of our men dismounted and I am one of that number. I dont know what they are going to do with us whether they will send us to the breastworks or remount us but think they will remount us. Some of the men think the prospects for peace are very good some of the boys told me last night that Jef Davis had give it up to Lee and Grant to settle but that he did long ago so that counts nothing to us. Still I hope that war will soon close I am tired and want to get home.

You spoke of Tap Hite preaching, wish that I could hear him but I hear no preaching nothing but cursing and swearing there is plenty of that day and night. I would like for the girls at home to write to me. If they can I want you to tell them for me that I nearly get out of patience some times and think they dont care for me. I shal have but little chance to write for there is going to be a hard summers work for us. The weather here is fine warm and nice but the wind blows to beat Texas making the sand fly all the time, the fruit trees are beginning to bloom.

Well Pleasy I some times get in the dumps and feel as if I dident care how things go then again I think of home and the loved ones and long to be there. I want to see the little hands that marked that letter, Tammy and Willy I can see but it only makes me feel sad to look at them. I sometimes think of sending the pictures home. I cant take very good care of them here then if the Johneys were to get me they might tare and stamp them in the ground before my eyes. Often do tears unbidden come when I look at them and think that I may never see their lively forms or hear their prattling tongues. Remind them of me, give my love to all and pray that we may meet again in this life and finaly in the world to come. I remain your loving Companion till death.

Joseph to E.P. Leatherwood

---

[19]   **Transcriber's note**: The girls at home, mentioned in Joseph's letters above, were his own sisters. Rod and Town, in the last letter above, were Rodney and Townsend Nichols, brothers of Emily. Adlaid and Sarah were siters of Emily, while Tam Newlon, another of her sisters, was the one for whom little Tammy was named.

Before the date of the next letter from Joseph, the Confederate army had surrendered. Joseph's regiment was sent to Missouri to await discharge. Perhaps it was largely because of the let-down after the war ended, but it is clear from the last of his letters that Missouri was not Joseph Leatherwood's favorite place: "No place like home."

20 Jun 1865 – Benton Barrack, Mo.

Dearest Plesy,

I take my pen once more to writ you a few lines just to let you know that I am still alive and in tolerable health and hope this may find you the same. The weather is very warm and makes it very uncomfortable in the Barracks and then we have very bad water and a heap of filth about the back streets. So upon the whole, it is a very unpleasant place to stay. Then to make the thing still worse about two thirds of the men are drunk most of the time. I think that I have saw as disgraceful sights here as ever I saw in my life, last night there was a part of 3 Regiments of infantry came in such a lot of drunken men I never saw.

Pleasy I am as near being homesick as ever I was. I suppose Major Easton is at home now there is thousands of rumors now in camp …

… there was some horse equipment that came in and now it is for Texas Mexico, the plains, Rocky Mt. and I cant tell where else. I get sick hearing such foolery. I would much rather hear something from home for I have not heard from there since I come here and it seems a very long time. I think this the most cramped up place that I ever saw, the place is infested with women pedling bread and vegetables (and some for other purposes) they will ask 5 cents for 5 onions or raddishes or half - a dozen cheries they know that such things are tempting to the soldier.   He gets tired of dry bread, coffee and fat meat and some little tastes good to him to him but he has to pay dear for them.

Well Pleasy I am writing a heap of letters but I have nothing else to do. I went to the photograph gallery today and engaged some pictures but I know you will scold when you get them but if they dont suit you you must …

… give them away, give some of them to the girls. Anyhow I look tough, feel tough and gess I am a little tough, I am a Soldier. Some think a soldier in not a man and many of them would Make you think so, if you could see their acts. But I feel the same manly pride that I did at home but I must stop for today. Candle light.

Pleasy I got your letter this evening but heard later than that for Jenkins come up this evening. I am going to try for a furlow dont know if I shal get it for they say we are going to Springfield, Mo. I would like to get my pay first but dont think there is much chance now. I think I should like to get away from here. If we dip a mess pan full of water and let it settle there is a half inch of the nastyest mud you ever saw in the bottom of it. There is so much confusion that I must stop. I want you to write often as you can. I got a …

… letter from Rod and Town since I got here. Are you sure that Saminas address is Elwin that is a singular name nothing more tonight so good night to you.

Good morning Pleasy this is a nice cool morning and I feel prety well. I believe there is nothing new this morning. Jef told me that you had planted the melon seed but I fear I shall not get to eat the melons this summerr, well now I shal close this poor letter hoping to hear from some of you soon. I remain your loving Compansion til death. Give my love to all even to Jack and Puss,

Joseph. to Emily P. Leatherwood

You must not get discouraged think I shal get home after a while.

28 Jun 1865 – Camp, 2nd OVC Near Rolla, Mo.[20]

Dear Pleasy,

I take up my pen this morning to inform you that I am still enjoying good health and hope this may find all of you in the same state of health. We left the Barracks on the 23 inst. and arrived at Rolla on the 24th. This is the poorest country that I have saw yet the land is very poor and the people look poorer. If there is no better place in Missouri than this I shal never migrate.

The teams are loading our stuff this morning for Springfield, MO. which is distant about 150 miles. This we will have to foot which will be a hard trip for men not used to walking. I suppose our business there will be to guard trains to Fort Smith and down in Arkansas. I dont think the duty will be so very hard if the weather dont be to hot. It is extremely hot here. By tracing the map you can see where we are.

I hope to get letters from some of you prety often. I wrote to Meek before I left Bladeneburg and if she got it I fear she has forgot it. I wrote to Kate since I come to St. Louis and hope to hear from her soon.[21] I got some pictures and started them home hope you shal get them. If they get through keep [of] them for yourself and the children and give the rest to those that may want them. I kept one for Samina, if I hear from her, I wrote to her but have got no ans. yet. I want you to tell me how you are.

Off for money, Friday is our muster day then I will have 10 months due me but cant tell when we will be paid. I hear that the goverment is going to stop paying any bounty only to those that serve out their time. Now if the thing is going to be worked in that way dont be surprised if I try to get home before my time is out for if it is going to fly the track I cant see that I am bound to stick.

Now there is a heap of stories here about our old friend Heistand and the folks at and about town. If there is any thing new just give me a little hint not so as to knock me down but so that I can understand. Some of you give me the news generally, I suppose you think that I ought to give you some news but I dont know a thing. We dont get a paper and if we do there is little or nothing in it.

Tell Pap when I get to Springfield I will try and write him a short letter if I can. Now I want you to write as often as you can. Once in 10 days any how three or four of you certainly can do that, hoping to hear soon. I will close. Give my love to all. I remain as ever your faithful and loving companion till death.

Farewell for the present, Jos. to Emily P. Leatherwood

I wrote a letter to Leah some time ago and have not heard from it yet. Direct your letters to Springfield, MO.

---

[20]   **Transcriber's note**: This letter is one I found among my mother's things. L.E.F.
[21]   **Transcriber's note**: Kate and Leah, mentioned above, were two of Joseph's sisters; Meck was his sister America, Sazanina (Nichois) Carpenter was one of Emily's sisters, the one who lived past age 100.

9 May 1865 – Letter to Joseph From Emily[22]

Editor's Note: *The subjects of the letter would indicate that it was written after the preceding letters from Joseph to his wife. It may be that she started the letter on May 9th.*

May the 9th

Well Joseph,

      I seat my self this plesant sabbeth Morning to inform you that we are all well at present and hope this may find you the same. I recived your letter you sent while at Rolla all so the one with the pictures, eleven of them. We was much pleased with them. Tammy knew them. Willey dident know them he was quite outdun when I told him (w)ho it was, to think he didenot know them. I gave each of your sisters one of them am going to give Rodnah and Tam one if they want sum. The rest I will keep awhile send that one on to Samina as you are moving you may miss hur. Hur and Gip rote to me last fall to send …

… them your addree I never sent it til you went to MO.

You sed you wanted me to giv you the news. I hant got eny to giv. I hant bin to town onley once in awhile to the store and to meeting once in to or three weeks, dont here much. As for our old friend Heistad I hant herd aney thing new. I wood like fore you to give me a hint of what you herd out there. He has bin very accomidating to me sence you left. If I want eney thing and hant got the money I can get it from Heistand without. I have 1 hundred dolers in the hous. I want to keep if I can. I lent Enos 20 dolers, I will get as soon as he is pade. He has one years pay coming to him. I never got but ten dolers from the co. I got an order fore ten more in May but there hant …

… eney money come in sence.   Goods has bin so hi sence you went away it tuck a heap to cloath us. I make as litel, do as I can. I wood like to save a litel if I can.   I will have three hogs to faten this fall, will have corn to try to faten them. Pap has a fine prospect fore corne.

You sed that you herd that the government was going to yank the men out of the bounty. The way I herd it they will get according to the time thay stay. I think that will be fare. I want you to come home as soon as you can get but never run of, tell them you are sick or that youre leg hurts and you can get a discharge. Solgers are coming home all the time the 1st O.V.H. (?) has got home all onley the new recruts and the boys that is at Covington.   Jos Heistands boys is at camp …

somethin else to talk about. If they ever sed any thing about me I dont know it. I dont care how much they talk if they tell the truth.

After a harty diner and a fine rain I hasten to close my pore leter my pen is worne out and I cant think to get one you must take care of youre self. Anna ses she is going to kiss papey when he comes. Nothing more but remain yure loving compasion till death farewell.

E.P.L.to Joseph Leatherwood

Since I finished my later Sara Kisling came and brot youre coat and blanfet the things was in the pocket. It seem, unlikely that Emily rated "A" in spelling, though she did havs plenty of small home news to tell.

To all whom it may Concern.

Know ye, That _Joseph Leuthenure_ a _Sergeant_ of Captain _Nathtillnure_ Company, (_L_,) _2_ Regiment of _Ohio Cavalry_ VOLUNTEERS who was enrolled on the _Ninth_ day of _April_ one thousand eight hundred and _Sixty first_ to serve _three_ years or during the war, is hereby **Discharged** from the service of the United States, this _12th_ day of _October_, 186_5_, at _Benton Barracks Mo_ by reason of _G. O. 74 C. I. War Dept_

(No objection to his being re-enlisted is known to exist.*)

Said _Joseph Leuthenure_ was born in _Columbiana County_ in the State of _Ohio_, is _Thirty six_ years of age, _Five_ feet _Eleven_ inches high, _dark_ complexion. _Blue_ eyes, _dark_ hair, and by occupation, when enrolled, a _Farmer_

Given at _Benton Barracks Mo_ this _12th_ day of _October_ 1865.

* This sentence will be erased should there be anything in the conduct or physical condition of the soldier rendering him unfit for the Army.

[A. G. O. No. 99.]

Nath Villnure
Captain Comd L, 2 Vol.

By 13 Mo. Cav. Vol,
Commanding the Regt.
Benton Brg, Mo,

Part III

The Civil War Letters as Transcribed by Lois Ellen Fenn

LETTERS WRITTEN BY WILLIAM H. LEATHERWOOD, UNION ARMY

Who enlisted in the 91st Ohio Volunteer Infantry
August 8, 1862.

Camp Portsmouth
August the 20th

I am still well. I got a little tuch of cold last night. It comes my time to stand gard to night, there was one gard run off last night, they put him on gard and he set his gun down and sloped. The Captain told me a little while ago that there was thirteen hundred men in camp. Well Jo, I was not as bad board as some of the boys thought I was in the Captain. He is second to none, he is no military man but he is as clever a man as I ever seen and is well thought of by all. We are looking for the Mustering Officer today. My feete are getting verry sore, my boots are to tight for mustering in. I dont know how long we will stay here. I wish you would gow down to the Grove and tell Sam Teener that I want him to make me a pare of boots, he has my measure. If you have any way of sending them down, you can find out whether any one is coming down or not, you had better not send down by the male for I never get to go out to town and it is so far out to camp that it would be a hard chance to get them, there is no telling how long we will stay here. I would like for you to come down if you can. We have amost every thing gowing on here, some pray, some sing, some sware and som play cards. Tell the girls that I have not got my uniform yet but as soon as i get it I will have my miniture taken and send it to them. But I must come to a close, tell Tommy and Willy that I would like to see them. Nothing more at present but remain your afectionate bother W. H. Leatherwood.

Rite and let me know how the folks are getting along, direct to 91st Reg. OVI Camp Portsmouth, Ohio, care of Captain Clark.

(Sam Teener, mentioned above, was what my mother used to call "a sort of cousin," several Teeners who were nephews of her great-grandmother having moved to Ohio from Maryland about the time her great-grandparents Zachariah and Catharine (Teener) Leatherwood did. - L.E.F.)

Camp Ironton
Sep. 11, 62

Dear Brother

It is with pleasure that I take my pen to let you know that I am well at present. Well I will begin by telling you my adventuers, we have been to Western Virginia and seen some of the efects of war. We got a dispatch that Old Jenkins was coming to Guyandott with about two thousands of men, we gathered up and started, there was six companies went up. We started night before last, we got up there just at day brake but the Rascals had left. There was Six Companies of the Second Virginia Cavalry there and as shure as you live they are a hard set of Boys but there is fight in them. It is a hard looking place, it showes the efects of war, the houses are burnt and the people look distressed. We wer on small rasions while we was there, the Cavalry boys laughed at us for not gowing and taking what we wanted, they say they have learned to take care of themselves. We was only there about ten hours then we came back. Jenkins was in Barbersvill seven miles up the Guyan River. Colonel Turly dident want to gowonith the armes we

have and I suppose that was the reson that we came back, we are to get
better arms today and then we will be apt to leave here. I rote Pap
a letter the other day about my money, I sent it to West Union to the
Bank. Him or you must go and get it, if you want any of it you are
welcom to it.

Well Jo I dont want to brag but when we got orders to march I was
the first in ranks, the Boys comensed taring around asking questions and
the Cap had hard work to get them in. It is not agreable to fight but
Jo I am not afraid to fight and Jo acording to your request I am trying
to be a good boy. I have had a good deal of enjoyment since I came in
camp, you may rest satisfied conserning me. Tell Em that I would like
to see her but to tell the truth I would rather see Tamm and Willy than
any body else, some times it seems to me that I would give amost any
thing to see them. But I must come to a close, tell the folks that i
am still on hand, I dont know where I will be when I wright again but
let me be where i will my trust is in God. Jo remember me in your prayrs
I expect this will be the last letter I will write here but I will write
again soon, you must wright and tell me how you are getting along.
Nothing more at present but remain your afectionate brother until death
William Leatherwood

Point Plesant
Sept the 21, 62

Dear Brother
It is with the gratest of pleasure that I take my pen this
Sabbath morning to let you know that I am well and harty. I received your
letter on Wensday and was glad to hear from home, nothing givs me more
pleasure than a letter from home. We are still here but have had no
fight and not much prospect of it just now. We left Ironton on last
Saturday week and I thought that i was gowing home, we started for Maysvill, we got the news that it was taken by a considerable forse of Rebles.
We all thought that we were gowing home to fight but alas we were all
disapointed, we only got as far as Portsmouth and then got the fun of
gowing back and a little further back than I agreed for i naturly hate
these poor Virginia hills, but here we are and cant help it. We thought
that we would have to march to Bufalow when we got here but thank Providence we dident. We had a hard trip up here, we had to lay on the hericon*
deck and you had better believe it was som hot thru the day and not so hot
at night as to pail ? the hide. We got off of the Boat about noon on
Sunday last and I was just sick enough to go and lay down in the shade,
laying in the hot sun on the Boat gave me the headache but as soon as I
got a drink of good watter i got better and today i feel as stout as a
buck. We have lots of company, there are seventeen Regiments here, there
are three Batteries of artillery and I guess about two Regiments of cavalry.

Well Jo I am getting along with the Boys verry well, i have got in
as good a mess as there is in the Company, the Boys came pretty ny having
a dispute about who should have me. I would have rote sooner but i could
not get paper, it is not home here I just have to write as the case will
admit of. I was out on picket night before last but it is a thing i
dont much hanker after it. This is a hard place the people are pretty
nere all secesh but I think again we leave here they will vote the Union
ticket. The farm our camp is on belongs to a Reble he is in the Reble
army, if we stay here a while longer he maby will find his land if he
gets back but that will be all. There is a man on the farm that says
he is Union, he raised corn but we are gathering it the cavalry boys
pitch in and take the hard corn and we take the rostenears. We have

*Hurricane deck?

got it about cleared out. We use the fence for cooking, the boys don't
forget to catch the chickens, they caut the last old hen this morning
and she had three little chickens. Colonel Turly says go ahead, he is
rite. Well Jo I will tell you about our grub, sometimes we get pretty
good and somtimes it is hard, we got some beef the other day that was
sort of how come you so and that wasent the first, but dont think I am
disatisfied I am better satisfied than i have ever been. Captain D---y*
give the quartermaster a cussing yesterday for not getting better grub
for his men. ̶X̶x̶x̶x̶x̶x̶x̶x̶x̶x̶x̶x̶x̶x̶x̶x̶x̶ Your letter encouraged me verry
much you said to look ahead, I have always don that if I had have looked
back i would have been dead befor now. I cant help thinking of home and
if it was not for home i would have nothing to encouriage me and if i
ever get into a fight and think of home the Rebles had better be agowing.
I could not help laughing when I read about Old Jacob gowing to make
them git, I was som surprised to here that Dock was Captain but I was
glad that the people down in old Adams were a waking up to a sense of
there duty. There is gowing to be somthing don, we got the news last
eighing that McClen had whiped Lee and taken Fifty thousand prisinors,
if that is true i think that it will play out after a while. I showed
the Captain your letter and he was much pleased with it, he said it was
worth reading, he said if it hadent bin that some of the other Boys wanting to get off he would have give me a transfer to Murphys Company. I
would have like very well to have been with them but i have friends here.
Jo I am still trying to live rite, I have to watch myselfe verry close
for there are all most evry thing to draw the mind off but i am still
on the way. I was sorry to here that the Boys that went to the Sixtieth
Regiment wer taken prisinors, I am afraid that there Six months will
turn out to be a long one. Tell the Friends that i would like to write
to all of them but it is imposible for me to do so, it is not like sitting down at home to rite a letter, i am under an Aple tree laying rite
flat down with a barl head for a desk. But i must come to a close by
saying that i wish you all well and hope that we will all meet once more,
give my respects to all enquiring friends tell Tammy and Willy that Uncle
Will wants to see them, tell Em that I send my love to her. Direct your
letters to Gallapolice Ohio nothing more at present

                         but remain your Mother *(? just what he wrote!)*
                         William H. Leatherwood

#Gallipolis
* Captain's name is not clear.

Point Pleasant, Va.
Oct. 8, 62

Dear Brother,
        it is with the gratest of pleasure that I take my pen
to let you know that I am well this morning I received your letter
yesterday and was verry glad to here from you we have made a little
move since I last rote. we have cosed [crossed] the Kanawha River
we was camped rite between the Ohio and the Kanawha, we are now on
the south of the Kanawha we are now in a Briggade the fourth and
thirteenth Va. the thirty fourth and 91 Ohio, comanded by Col.
The General is Gilmore. Well Jo I have got over my scare that I
got up at Bufalow.

    I was glad to here that you making the Bulls git, just pitch
into them if i was at home i would like to have a company of bulls
if i dident make them trot it would be curious. there is a considerable forse here and more acoming there will be somthing done in
western Va. before long. Jo i tell you i dont like the ide of wintering
in these hills but if the rest can stand it Billy can. I am as harty
as ever i was but it is not on acount of the fine things that we have
to eat we have had no soft Bread only what we bought, we have crackers
and baken rice and beans and some beef that we captured at buffalow
but i can do very well as long as i keep well i can go it. You said
you was not gowing to sow any wheat until it raind, if things look
there like they do here I dont think you will, not some day soon for
it is wonderful dry here but you have enough to do you anyhow.

    Well I dont know how soon the war will be over but i hope it will
be over in time for me to get home next winter. Jo we have as good an
old Colonel as any other Reg. in the service he haint above speaking
to any of us. you wanted to know the letter of our Co. it is Co. E.
I fancy i could see you setting down making bulets to shoot the devlish
Rebles but I must close you must wright if you cant rite much rite a
little it dose me good to here from home if it haint but three words.
Tell Em i am still the same Billy i think of little Tammy and Willy
evry day. Recolect the letter is E, 91 Reg. nothing more at present
but remain yours as ever

                William Leatherwood.

                Gauley Bridge, Va.
                Nov. 5th 62

Dear Brother,
        it is with grate pleasure that I rite you a few lines
to let you know how I am getting along the Lord is blessing me with
excelent helth I am growing fat on hard crackers baken and beens.
I got your letter yesterday and it was a welkim visitor. it was with
me like it was with you I hadent got any letter for some time but I
wasent uneasy i knowed there was some acoming.

    we have the pleasure of staying here at Gauley on the hill side
it is some of a job to get wood and watter it is snowing to day but
I am in the tent verry well satisfied to let it snow. you said that
you felt for the soldiers i dont doubt that but I havent suferd much
since i have been out i havent stood guard for over a month i was on
fatigue duty once. iaam verry well off for cloths i have two pare of
pants and two woolon shirts overcoat dress coat blouse two pare of
good socks and one not so good i bought me a pare of gloves (sheep

skin) of the best kind grait long fellows my boots are good yet.
i was glad that you rote some war news that is somthing we dont get
much on. i let some of the boys read it they said it was good we
all try to beleive one item in it that was that the war will be over
soon. I supose the Boys of the Sixtieth are glad they are alive
well i dont begrudge them the pleasure of home. the news of the
change of Burnside and Rosecrans we think that the war will close
that much sooner. we will move soon we will go to Fayetteville
it is about fifteen miles from here over Cotten Mountain we are
good to winter in the hills the 117 has got a good place. there
are a heepe of barking here from cold it sounds distressing to
wake up of a night and heer the coffing. we lay on the ground
i have some cold but none to hurt. Well Billy would like to go
home and stay about two weeks but he dont let that trouble his mind
much.

        Jo I am getting along with the Boys verry well. i havent saw
a woman for some time. you must not think that i dont write to you
i write evry week i dont want any thing from home aithout it is your
prayers if you can i would like to have some postage stamps send
only a few at a time. i must close for the present write soon
tell Enos Newland to tell me how he liked it tell the boys that i
haint homesick yet tell Em and the girls that i send my love to them
and I wouldent forget Pap and the little children i would like to see
you all. I still remain yours
                                        Will Leatherwood

                                        Nov. 19, 1862

        Well Jo I am up here at Galley (Gauley) at last and it is a
hard place I am well all to my back I got it hurt and I will tell
you how I done it i was detailed to guard the Battoes # with provisions and the hands all left and i had to stay and work and pushing
on them i hurt it but it will be all rite in a day or too. I was
away from the Reg. fifteen days and when i came to camp the   ys
made as big a fuss as tho i had bin gone a month but i will pass.
i got yours and Cates letters and was glad to here from home i have
not riten as often as i would like to have done i never got to Gauley
until mondy it is a hard looking placess soon as the sun gets up it
begins to go down i dont think we will stay all winter i think we will
go farther up or down there are a lot of soldiers in the Valley we
are comanded by General Scammon we never here of the Rebles any more
a news paper is a rarity here you wanted to knowwhat kind of guns
we have we have the Austrian Rifel they shoot well we have Caps and
you wanted to know how i was fixed when that night it snowed. I was
at a little Creek called Pokey we made a sort of a shelter but i got
wet and tuck a bad cold but it dident hurt me much. them old Bankers
are a getting mity fresh i should like to here of them being taken
down. you wanted to know whether i wanted any thing i have no use
for money for there is nothing tobbye if i had plenty of it. Still
have some I want you to write whether you got my money or not if you
can i would like if you would send me some ostage Stamps.
        I must close tell Em that i send my love to her and the children
i blieve that is all at present I remain yours as ever

                                        Billy to Joseph Leatherwood

Battoes - small flat-bottomed river boats (bateaux).

Fayetteville, Va.
December 28, 62

Dear Brother,

this pleasent Sabbath day finds me seated in a nice cabin. I have just come off of guard i was out on picket but dident get to see nary Reble i was on the out post it is pretty hard to stand on the out post we are not alowed to sleep any i got pretty sleepy last night. I am well and harty it is as nice a day as ever I saw for this time in the year we have got our winter quarters done at last if they let us stay here this winter we will have a good time of it.

Well Jo the news are rather discouraging here i hardly know how to take it you know that i never believed any thing till the last pinch but Old Burnside is whiped and no mistake. Some of the boys are getting verry much discouraged they say we will never whip the Rebles it does look rather spurious. some of them say they would like to here that they had comprymise so they would get to go home, they would rather go home than save there country i dont look at it that way yet I would like to be at home verry well but i would rather do the fighting and then come. the Boys are getting Furlows i dont know whether i will get one or not i believe if i can get one for twenty days i will come home it would not give me much time to stay but if i only stay a week it would be verry much satisfaction to me but i dont flatter my self with the idea of one but after some of the maried men get them i will stand as good a chance as any of them. the pay master has not come yet we are looking for him soon if he comes and i get a furlow i would be in town they are beginning to make out the pay rolls then Uncle Sam will owe us four months pay it would cost me about ten dollars to come home. I would freely give it just to see you all i would give that just to see the children. this is the dogondest place that ever i saw there is hardly any buddy lives here and what does are the meanest people that ever the Lord let live they cant look at a man. it is here like it allways is they just let them come in and go out just as they please almost buti must close write soon and often give my love to all Yours truly

                                        Billy to Joseph Leatherwood

                                        Fayetteville, Va.
                                        January 5, 63

Well Jo, your letter has just come to hand I was glad to here from you that you were well but was sorry to here that you had the dumps so, but you must not let it get you down So it may be that it will all work out rite yet I knew that them Democrats would get sassy after the election i am as hard on them as ever but it wont do to talk about that here i am like old John Keesling i think that if trators was cleaned out in Ohio that the war would close sooner. to tell you the truth i dont expect if live to come home for three years that is to stay the way things look now we stand a good chants to stay out three years and then volunteer again i know one that wont go again i did think for a while that the thing would stop some time but i wouldent say now how long it would last. we here some of the biggest news that you ever herd the boys are all getting tired of it they are all complaining. Jo it is my opinion that this war will never be closed honerable i have an idea that the

Southern Confederacy will acknowledge at last. Well Jo I am some
like you i think untill we get better officers we will never gain
the day i still think that Old Abe means well but he is in a tite
place. there was awful news here about Burnsides defeat i never
know how to take any thing when i here it in short to tell you
what i think of it i think it is a bad egg. I am not home sick
yet but i do think it could be managed better i am getting along
very well the Boys are very good to me and the officers are also
good to me our Old Colonel cant be beat he is clever and kind to
his men but Old Scammon is a real old scoundrel he makes the Boys
take there hats off when they meete him I have never had the honor
of that though i have ben on gard at his quarters you said that
the 117 was steeling if the Goverment will only send them up here
they never will be disbanded for steeling for they couldent find
any thing to steel. that young Aston is a deserter he left when we
started from the Point he had better keep scarce or he will be
fetched back and it wont be so funney as gowing home was. Jo you
said that you dident know whether your letter would interest me or
not you may rest easy about that just give me plenty of such any
thing from home dose me good. I never think of such a thing as
desertion it has plaid out with me but i am gowing to stick to it
till the last cat is hung. Jo I am sorry that you have to lose your
rights i think that Old Ned has payd # the rascal out and out if
there is any of my money left you take it and use it we are looking
for the paymaster and then i will send you some more you are as welcome to it as if it was your own we will never quarl about it.
there are still some of the boys gowing home i dont know whether i
will get to come home or not if the pay master dont come it will be
hard for me to make the trip there is no dificulty in a citizen
coming here there is some comes from Adams here you could come to Piat
on a boat Camp Piat twenty five miles below the bridge then it is
twelve miles here the trains are gowing all the time to Piat if you
think of coming up i want you to let me know if i dont get to come
home i will pay your way if you will come it will only cost about
ten dollars to come and go here. I must tell you about the dreme i
had last night i drempt that i saw Willy but i thought he was a
corpse i felt bad over it untill i got your letter to day.
language can not tell how well i would like to see them it dose me
good to here that they have not forgot me yet. I was sorry to here
that James McClure was dead but we must all die one day or an other.
I must close soon you must write as often as you can dont think
you will worry my pacience writing so much write about every thing
i will not know for a month or so whether i will get to come home or
not then i will write to you and if you can come up i would be glad
that is if i cant come home it will pay you to come and see the country. i believe that is all i can think of now so i will close by
saying that i wish you all well i send my love to you all yours in
love

                    William Leatherwood

    i will send your letters without paying the postage then you
need not send so many i only want some to send a letter to some one
else.

Fayetteville, Va.
Febuary 16, 63

Dear Brother,

once more I take my pen to inform you that I am well.
I received your letter on Saturday and on Sunday I had to go on
guard so I could not answer it sooner I was glad to here from you
there is a hi old time here today the pay master has been here and
payed us off and the Boys are lyting out like sheep. there was
thirty or forty of the thirty fourth Boys went since Saturday there
several of the twelfth and some of the ninty first, they are gowing
evry chance they get it looks like the war would stop some time when
all the soldiers desert then I guess it will stop. I had a visitor
last week it was old Sammy Dempsy one of his sons is in the second
Va. Cavlry and he come up to see him and he came in to our camp to
see me. he says he thinks the war will stop about June or July I
hope it will. Jo you spoke of gowing to the Army, you just stay at
home as long as you live if you haint forsed to go it is no fun
and you just stay there. The Boys in the 117 are playing hob they
will be a little carful how they do it after this.

you have had more snow down there than we have had up here we
have had rite smart rain the mud is verry deep I just came off guard
this morning our company went after the deserters but they wont get
any of them there is two companyes out of our Regiment to look after
them there is two companies gon to Summers Ville to guard provisions
and clothing it is thirty five miles up Gauley above the Bridge.
we are getting scatterd rite smart. there is strong talk of our Regiment beeing mounted if we are then we will see service we are gowing
to get new guns we are gowing to get the Springfield Rifels then when
we get an old poor horse then we will cut a big hog in the Ass, for
my part it dont suit me verry well but it pleases me verry well that
we are gowing to get new guns the ones we have are not much acount
they shoot like all the world but they dont shoot with any certanty.
we have hard bread and pork that is two or three years old beens
have played out but we are fat yet.

Well I told you that the paymaster had been here and payed us
off I got just forty nine dollars and I owed the Sutler four dollars
and sent thirty five home I have eleven and a quarter left we all
sent our money with the paymaster to Columbus ahd you can get it at
West Union I will send the receipt in this letter and you or Pap I
had it put in his name but he can go to the County Auditor and he
will give you an order to the County Tresurer and he will give you
the money. that was the onley way we had to send it and it is as
safe as any if the receipt gets miscarried the Captain has it to
show that I did send it and I can get it still. if you want any
of it take it and use it you are welcom to it go as soon as this
comes to hand and get it. I asked Dempsy about it he sayed it was
safe.

Well I guess that is all now you just stay at home if you know
when you are well I would like to se you but I have come to the
conclusion that it wont pay you to come up here you couldent have
much satifaction. well I guess that I have told you all that I
can think of this time so I will have to close you must write soon
and tell me whether you got this or not. tell Em that i haint

forgot her yet tell the folks that I am allIrIte yet and have no
notion of deserting I send my respects to all the friends and
love to all the Family no more but remain your brother and friend

                            William Leatherwood

Direct to Fayetteville, Va. Co. E, 91 Regiment

                                    Camp Reynolds, Va.
                                    March 25, 63

Dear Brother,
            once more I take my pen to let you know Lhat I am
well at present I received your letter on the twenty first and
was glad to here that you wer all well. we are camped on the bank
of the Kanawha River just below the falls it is a nice place far
more so than where we was but I dont know how long we will stay
here there is two Companies at Summers Ville and there is two more
gowing to the Bridge and there is talk of some more gowing to Loup [Loop]
Creek I expect that ours will go next the 91st will soon be no
Regiment at all in was counted the best Regiment in the Service
from Ohio at least old Davie Tod says so it has the most men for
service than any other. the River is verry high today we have
butlittle news here and I expect it is for the better. I was glad
to here that my receipt had got home I was a little afraid it
would not go safe I saw in one of the County papers whare Pap
had got the money
      Well, Jo, I must tell you what I think of the Conscript I
think it is all right I have an idea that it will make som of
them Secesh git up and dust it is a verry tight law as you sayd
but not any to tight for some it has encouraged me some. Some of
the Boys sayd that it would make war at home but I never thought
so if it was to I would like for Co. E to go to Adams to help it
along. Lieutenant Croford has returned he says the People are
more reconsiled than they was he is well again the Boys done a
good job at Columbus. the talk is that the Rebles are leaving
Vixburg if they let them run off I dont know what ought to be
done with them but anything to keèp the war gowing on I am
anxious to here of something being done. I do hope that the
people at home will do the thing that is right and the war will
be over a graideel sooner but I am gowing towrite to Cate I will
have to close this I want you to rite as often as you can and
give me the news of the day. give my Love to Emily and the
Children no more but remain your Loving Brother

                            W.H. Leatherwood

                                    Summers Ville Va.
                                    May 7, 63

Dear Brother
            this morning I take the opportunity of informing
you where I am we are at Summersville we left Camp Reynolds
Sunday the third and got here the fourth I was so sore and
tierd that I could not write I am well we made thirty two
miles in one days time I was one of the first in we are getting
farther from home and closer to the Rebs there is no telling when

we will have a fight here but they will find the 91st here when
they come. Jo I would rather be at home helping plant corn this
morning. Sunday night I laid on the wet ground and it rained in
my face it made me mad we had to wade several Creeks in fact it
haint any fun to be a Soldier. this looks more like living than
any place we have been for six months but there haint herdly any
boddy lives here and nothing hardly to live on I hardly think we
will stay here verry long and of corse dont know where we will go.
we may go to Clarksburg or down the Valley the Cavlery went out to
Louisburg the other day and as usal they herd they was comming
twentyfour hours before they got there and they was prepared for
them and licked them out the news goes here rite fast to the Rebs
but none to us they are all Rebles here they know anything quicker
than we do if I had my way about it I would kill evry devvle of
them then we could do something. the Regiment is all here there is
good brest works here for Infantry we have no Artilery here just
Rifle pits if they dont fetch Artilery here we will give them some
fun. I cant write much now as I have to write with a pencil on
my knee I dont know whether you can read this or not but if we
stay here I will write you one you can read. this is to let you
know that I am alive if I had a good place to write and a pen
and ink I would give you a full description of the march and the
country but I will do that when I get home but to close tell Em,
Tammy and Willy that Uncle Will still thinks of them and would
like to see them I give my love to all the family still direct
to Charleston nothing more this time still remaining yours
as ever

                                        W. H. Leatherwood

                          Gauley Bridge Va.
                          May 15, 63

Well, Jo, this morning I take my seat on the ground with my paper
on my knee to write you a few lines I am seated on the hill side a
above the Bridge I am well I wrote to you when we was at Summerville
but it was only a few lines we got up there on the fourth and
started back on the ninth so that our stay was short. it was a
hard march up there and harder coming back we made thirty two miles
in thirteen hours I hardly know what was the idea for going up
there without it was to have an excuse to hall a lot of grub up
there for the Rebles to get we was ordered away and everything
there and when we got here there was two trains ordered up to get
the grub and only a part of a company of Cavelry to guarde it and
the Rebles was wide awake and they waited untill the train got evry
thing and started back and they pitched in captuerd the hole thing.
the most of the Cavelry got away one Lieutenant and some of the
men wer taken it was the biggest Roar that ever I herd of. it looks
to me like old Scammon just sent it up for the Rebs if they had
burnt up evry thing and the town they would not have lost much but
the way it is they lost a lot of good muels and waggons. the Rebles
are reported to be in forse there I dont know whether we will go up
there or not. it was the intention for us to go to Parkersburg
when we came here and I dont know where we will go now. Well, Jo,
we herd some good news the other day but it turned out to be a hoax.

the news was that fighting Jo had taken Richmond   the news are
in our favor and I hope that they will take it yet   we haint had
much mail here since we left I havent had a letter from home for
a long time   I am anxious to here from home and how things are gowing
on there   I told you when I got some place where I could I would
write you the right kind of letter   I shant call this that one for
this is as mean a place to write as ever I saw. I cant write much
at best and to take it on my knee I cant do anything   I want you
to write soon and give me the news at home. I can not write much
this time all that I can tell is that we are at Gauley Bridge and
dont know where we will go next   So I will close for this time
give my love to all   write soon   I still remain yours as ever

                                    Will Leatherwood
I am out of stamps

                                    Gauley Bridge, June 15th 63
Dear Brother
                this extremely hot day I take my pen to let you
know that I am well and dooing well   I have been looking for a
letter from you for some time   and thought I would get one today
shure but it dident come so I thought I would write one more to
you. the weather is warm here the days are hot and the nights are
cool it is a healthy place here the deauty is heavy I go on picket
evry fourth night we are not allowed to have any fier or sleep any
it goes rite hard with me to keep awake all night but it dont go
as hard now as it youfed to. the news are tolearable good but not
as good as I would like anything short of Vixburg dont soot me
I still think that Grant will take it but it is too long acoming.
the Boys are all well pleased with the way they are deeling with
traitors in Ohio they haint hard enough for me if they had killed
Vallandingham and some more of his kind then it would pleas me.
Well Jo I hardly know how to write to you as there is nothing to
write   you know more about how things are gowing on than I do
I dont know what to think of war   some of the Boys think it wont
last long but I think it wont stop soon we haint bothered much here
with Rebs the reason is they are ordered other places. it will come
our turn some day they say they are gowing to make us get this fall
they will have a good time of it I recon. some of them Rebs at
home think there is an abbolition war now since the niggers are
helping to put the Rebellion down it is just the thing for me.
well it must close some time and I dont care how soon. it is just
ten months to day since we went into camp and I am better satisfied
than I was then I dont think as much about home the Boys all
treat me well and Gauley is my home. I want you to write and tell
me how things are gowing at home I expect you are buisy now but
it wont take you long some Sunday to write a few lines. Jo I would
like to be there and help you to harvest but it would go hard with
me to work now I have got so

        (bottom part of page torn off here)

that I am still alive I never had better health in my life I am
gowing to send two dollars in this and tell Em to buy Tammy and
Willy something to remember me by   I would have sent some home
but we only gottwo months pay and I thought it wouldent pay you
to go after it but I must close for this time write soon as you
can give my respects to all the friends and especily to the family
yours truly
                                    W. H. Leatherwood to his
                                    beloved Brother Joseph

(West Virginia separated from Virginia and was admitted to the
Union as a separate state June 20, 1863.)

                              Gauley Bridge, West Va.
                              June 29th, 1863
Dear Brother
            this hot day I once more attempt to rite you a few
lines to let you know that I am still alive and well things are
about as usual only our men had a little fight with the rebs the
other day at Loup Creek there was twenty four men out of the four
Companies that are here sent under command of Lt. Crofford to guard
the wharf boat six out of Co. E. the distance from here is six
miles they thought they would make a dash in there there was two
Cos. of the Second Va. Cavelry sent from Piat to meet them if they
did come but when they got up there instead of putting out pickets
they all laid down and went to sleep and the Rebs come on them
surprised and would have captured all of them if it hadent been for
our Boys but Lieutenant Crofford orderd them to fier which they done
with a good effect they hoisted five out of there saddles our Cavelry broke and run they all escaped but thirtyfive they wer captured
all ther horses and most of ther arms hone of our Boys wer hurt.
the firing was done across the River that is the way they do it up
here they watch untill they get a chance at some weak place and then
make a dash but if our men had kept a good lookout they would have
made them sorry for that but so it goes. Well the next thing is some
else the Pay master has been here for instance and give us our
rations of green backs we was paid for two months and I sent some
more home the pay agent dident come this time to take our money
home we all sent it to Galliapoliss and there check to West Union.
Pap can draw it at the Bank it haint as nice a way as we sent before but it was the best we could do I sent thirty three dollars
go as soon as you can and get it I received two letters from you
last week but thought I wouldent write untill I knew how the money
would go. one of your letters was almost out of date it was rote
on the 23rd of May some of them a long time a coming. I recon
them Rebles are cutting a big dash down there well evry dog has
his day there time will come some of these days to go up and they
will go up too mind if they dont. there will be some more after
a while to do like Ean did that was good. Jo you said you had a
notion to enlist just take a fools advice and stay at home as long
as you can the war has only comenced and when I get home I will relieve you and then you can go. the news from the East is not verry
good there haint much from below. Jo the way soldiers have to do
up here   ?   verry plesant I go on picket evry fore or five days
and some times oftener set up all night and not sleep a wink. as
far as the deauty is concerned I would rather be in front of Vixburg the privates go on evry other day the bush whackers ar getting
thick here again they are the devlishest set of men in the world
it is dangerous on picket but we have got so we dont mind it much
well Jo as I have no paper that is fit to rite on and not much to
rite about I will have to close and rite again. rite to me and let
me know whether you get the money if I was at home I could tell you
a heap but I am here and expect to stay till the war is over or till
my three years are up at any rate. I have just received a letter
from America # I was sorry to here that Cate # is sick I hope she
will get well soon I would rite more but the paper is so bad that
I cant rite it is a helthy a place here as I could get to. mind
that money will be sent to the bank you will have to receipt for it
#His sisters America (then 20) and Catherine (21)

I would have sent more but I bought a watch something that I
couldent do without and kept a little I believe that is all this
time write as soon as you can give my love to Em and all the rest
nothing more at present excuse my awkward way of writing I am not
advancing as fast in writing as I am in other things if I live
till this war is over it will be the best school that ever I went
to good health and long life to you all Good bye

                                        W. H. Leatherwood

                                        Gauley Bridge, West Va.
                                        July 7th 1863

Dear Brother
            yours of the 28th came to hand in due time and I was
glad to here from home the weather is still warm there has been rite
smart of rain here at least I thought so yesterday and last night
when on a picket post it rained for about two hours last night as
hard as ever I saw it I was on the hill just above camp in an open
field I had to stand and take it there is no such thing as running
to shelter her if it hadent been for my gum blanket I would almost
have drowned but as it was I didnt get much wet but for all it was
verry disagreeable. the news are good if what we here is true it is *
glorious both east and South I am afeard that it is to good to be
true but I will wait the truth of it. it done me good to here how
the Boys stick up to the Butternuts it would have done me good to
have heard that they had killed old Ned if I had been there with my
Springfield I could have shot him with as good grace as I could a
Reble up here I do hope the Boys wont let them go on as they have
been dooing I am glad to here that the Boys are still showing a
willing mind by enlisting and helping us clean the Confederacy out
I still believe we will do it but dont know how long it will take us.
you spoke of the Boys wanting you to go now Jo I dont want you to
go if you can help it I dont see how they could get along at home
without you and if they could it wont suit you it goes hard with me
to stay away from home a year and if you was to go and leave your
little children you would want to see them more than once before you
would get to but if you do dont go in the Infantry it is the hardest Service there is go in with the 117 if you must go that is gowing
to be a good birth for the boys I wish I was there I would like to
have you with me verry much but it wont suit you as well here as there
they wont have to stand guard like we do dont go as long as you can
help it. I wont say any thing about when the war will be over I
have my own opinion about it I got booth of your letters they was
one a long time a coming I got Enoses # letter but didnt answer
rite away and got word that he was gon and did not know how to direct
to him give me his address I let some of the Boys read your letter
they say that brother of mine is rite in the head well Jo I would
rite you a long letter if there was any thing to rite about. I
should like to see you all verry well I must close soon I will have
tosend this without a stamp as I am just out write again soon my
health is good I believe that is all this time give my love to all
no more but remain your true friend and brother

                                        W. H. Leatherwood

Enos Newlon, son of Tamzen (Nichols) Newlon, Emily's sister, who
lived in the home neighborhood. (Name is sometimes spelled Newland.)

 * The good news was of Vicksburg and Gettysburg both July 4.

[In the next letter Will teases Joe about Morgan's visit to
southern Ohio. On July 4, 1963, not aware that Gettysburg and
Vicksburg were both lost, General Morgan crossed the Ohio into
eastern Indiana, met some resistance, but turned east and swept
across southern Ohio in what was chiefly a nuisance raid, taking
food and horses as he went. At the Leatherwood farm some of his
men took "Trim," the favorite saddle horse, frightened the girls
and made them angry by taking "Pap" (aged 56) as well as Joseph
some distance down the road at an uncomfortable pace. Tammy and
Willy half remembered the incident, but their aunts never tired
of telling the story to them and later to their younger brothers
and sister. Morgan was captured in southeastern Ohio, and as
Will mentions, some of the Union troops in West Virginia were
sent to take care of the stragglers. R.E.J.]

                                    Fayetteville, Va.
                                    August 14th 63
Dear Brother
            your letter came to hand in due time but as I had
just rote to Kate I thought I would not answer for a few days
and as this just makes me one year in the Service of Uncle Sam
I thought I would write you a few lines. I am well the wether is
warm and we are drilling some and fortyfying in a week or too
this place will be hard to get at the Rebs will have some fun
before they get it they haint bothering us as much as they did
Colonel White is is command here he is a bulley old fellow he
can talk with a private as well as an officer. Well Jo I recon
you dont want to soldier any more when old Morgan is in command
he drills new recruits rather hard I shouldent like to be under
him myself he did play hob generaly but he is done now for a while.
I couldent help laughing when I heard how they got you drawn in
I can imagine how you felt when they made you give up your gun
but that was nothing if they had only left Trim you run a resk
and a grait one to following them if they had got you again you
would have went up the spout. I am sorry that I dident get to
see some of you that followed up but there was a poor chance to
get to see any one we was on the move all the time when we was at
Buffington I heard that the Seventh Ohio Cavelry was up the River
a mile or too I started to go up but when I got pretty near there
they had gon on a scout we was only there about four hours I would
have liked to have saw the Boys the best in the world but a soldier
cant have his way in such things it may be that we will get to see
each other some time I have an idea we will stay here all winter
again if we do and I dont get to come home I want you to come up
here. there haint been much news here for a few days the last
was faviarable from Charleston it is here just like it used to be
at home they all say now when we get a certain place then the war
will be over and as soon as we get it then there is an other. my
opinion is it wont stop

     (bottom part of page torn off)

if it is so pretty I want to see it give my love to all nothing
more but remain yours as ever
                                    W. H. Leatherwood

Fayetteville, West Va.
Sept. 25

Dear Brother,

After a delay of some days I will try to write you a
few lines your letter came to hand in due time but we was under
order to go on out post duty for ten days and I had no time to answer before we went and dident take any paper to write on so I had
to wait untill I came back. I am well it is raining some today the
Boys are all in good spirits, the news are not so good as they have
been the report is that Old Rosey has got a thrashing I am afraid
it is true. Jo I am sorry to here that the people are gowing so mad
in political matters, it is the worst thing for us that could be we
are all or nearly all a unit for Brough, there are some in the Regiment that will vote for Vallandingham but I dont think that there is
one in our Company the Val men are few and far between I am astonished
to see free Americans act so. I showed your letter to some of the Boys
and it pleased them well one of them red it and then asked me if he
mite read it to the mess I toled him he mite he red it and the Boys
all said you was all rite. I was sorry to here that you was not stout
but it is a consolation to know that you are where you can take care
of your self. well Jo I think that you had better make one trip up
to West Va. this winter it will pay you to come I want you to go to
Old Sam Tener and get him to make me a good pare of boots for this
winter and if you can come I would like for you to bring them up also
my over coat and a vest. I am not certain whether I can come home
this winter or not I wont need them things for a month or more but
have them made rite away. I have been looking for a letter from home
for a few days now and when I here how Leah is I will know more about
it I can get a ten day furlow after a while but I couldent more than
go and come in that time if she gets better I will not come for a
while if I dont come I would like for you or Pap one to come up and
see me it shant cost you anything to come only your time. There is
nothing of interest gowing on here so I will close for the present I
will tell you what I will do in my next if you cant come I will let
you know how you can send them, nothing more will write soon yours
truly

                              W. H. Leatherwood

                              Fayetteville, West Va.
                              Oct. 1st 63

Dear Brother,

your letter was received and read with grait interest
it found me in the best of health and tolerable spirits the news we
here is considerable mixed up there haint much information to be
got from them. there seems to be more Politics than any thing else
the people must be gowing wild they act as though there was nothing
else gowing on they dont think of the war any more at least it dont
look so to me. instead of trying to put it down they are trying to
make more, if they had to play soldier a while they would forget
their politicks. I tell you there hant much quarling among the soldiers they are about all of the same opinion. the Pay master has
made us another visit and give us two months pay I am gowing to send
some money home this time the pay agent was here this time and caried

our money home for us I am gowing to send my receipt in this and you
can get the money at West Union it is the best and safest way to send
it our clothing bill was settled this time I am sending thirty dollars if you get me a pair of boots pay for them out of it and if
you get in the notion of commong up take what will pay your way
I shall not try to come home for a while well I believe I have written all that is nessary all the news we get is in the papers and
you get them before we do we have the forts all done the probability
is that we will stay here this winter there is something gowing on
here. you must write as often as you can the Boys when I get a letter want to know if it is from my brother and if it is they want to
read it. tell Willey he must not grow so big that Uncle Will wont
know him I would give one months wages to see him and Tammy give
my love to all the family nothing more at this time yours as ever

                        Will Leatherwood

                    Fayetteville, West Va.
                    October 26, 63
Well Joseph, this morning I will write you a few lines to inform you
that I am well your letter was received and read with grait interest
I am truley glad your dream did not turn out as you thought it would
I never had better health than I have had this fall but it may not
last long. the Election went off all rite here the Adams County boys
done the clean thing for Brough but there was some traitors in this
Regiment there was seven in the 91st shame on such beastly ignorant
things in the shape of men I here that the Citizens elected the Union
ticket I say bully for Old Adams the Boys are all well pleased with
the result. we are working on our winter quarters have them about
half done it has been the talk for some time that we will go away but
I hardly think we will if we go any where it will be out to Louisburg
to clean them out of there that is sixty miles from here if we go
we will come back here to winter there is a Company out of the Briggade
out scouting they destroyed a large amount of property for the rebs
at the Sulpher Springs the other day. I am sorry you did not get my
Boots in that box but if you cant send them I can get along without
them we are having ameeting here now there was preaching last night
it makes me think of home to here a Sermon I was sorry to here of
them Brave Boys loosing there lives down there in the late battle
that was a grait Slaughter. I got a letter from Frank Messinger he
was in front nearly all the time he said Stone River was nowhere to
it. well Jo I have allmost give up the idea of this war closing any
ways soon at least during my term of enlistment and dont know as I
shall ever get home or not they are slow giving furlows I believe I
have told you all I can think of now I cant write much at a time without telling one thing over so often. I cant tell how well I would love
to see all of you I would like for you to come up but if you cant get
time dont come I am gowing to send you a kind of a report of the way
the election went a full report of the two Adams Co. Companies you will
see the 91st has the most traitors in the Brigade four of them from
Scioto County Co. C. but I must close for this time write soon
give my love to all the family yours as ever
                        Will Leatherwood

Since writing there has a furlow come for Billy Moore he lives
in West Union he has got a sick furlow he will stay twenty days or
he has a furlow for that time and I will send this by him with an
other   I have it wont do me any good here it may be of some
use some day   thats all

                                    Fayetteville, West Va.
                                    December 27th 63

Dear Brother,
                your welcome sheets was received on last evening and w
was read with grait interest I must tell you what I was doing I was
seated on my bunk watching the Boys roast a big gobler we had a rite
time over him the weather is bad it is raining to day this has been
a dry Christmas to me some of the Boys got whiskey and had a drunk
but that was no fun to me. we have just herd what our last raid on
Lewisburg was for it was to draw the attention of the Rebs while General Averill cut the Rail road he has done it all right and got out
safe. well I should love to see them trembling sinners their time is
almost up they will soon know what there doom is if it only takes the
rite ones then I will be satisfied but it is as like to take good
men as them traitors. the news are good so far as I have heard some
of the Boys are fanc(y)ing the war will close next summer but I cant
see it in that light I hope it will for if there was ever a boy sick
of any thing it is me of this cruel war there is still talk of us
gowing down on the River I would rather stay here as we have the best
quarters in the Valley but they just say go and we go the Soldiers
life is rather a hard one some times I get discouraged and dont care
for any thing and then I get over that but dont get in the notion of
dooing like them lads in tha artilery that is just what I expected
of such Soldiers if I herd the truth and I think I did that was that
they voted for Vallandingham, couldent expect any thing better. I
was glad to here that you had got your crib done I would love to come
home and see you all this winter but I cant tell whether I will or
not they are giving some furlows but the married men go first and
that is rite I would not ask for one untill they go. well Jo I cant
think of any thing to write about and will close my head is verry
foggy today tell Kate that I wil write to her soon give my love
to all I still remain yours as ever

                                    Will Leatherwood

                                    Fayetteville, West Va.
                                    January 19th 64

Dear Brother Jo,
                your letter bearing date of the ninth was received
last evening although it was short it was read with much interest
long letters are not always the best. the weather is cold today
our Company just came off of three days picket last evening the
weather was rather pleasant while we were out but since we came in
it has frozen up and now it is snowing. you spoke of the cold weather and wanted to know how I got along it has been verry cold here
since newyear at least part of the time I was on deauty Sunday after

newyear but did not suffer any from the cold I can stand more
than I use to and have plenty of clothes Uncle Sam clothes us
well if we dont get much else all I have suffered this winter was
when we went to Lewisburg I did suffer then it rained so much and
was so cold we had to wade several creeks. there is no news here
of importance to write more than you get in the papers. the Boys
are all well you have the start of me you can write about the weddings that are gowing off there is nothing of that kind goes off
up here I am glad they are still willing to make soldiers if they
wont come and be Soldiers them selves but there are butternuts
enough now. if I mistake not there will be a surprise party before
a year rolles around that will surprise them more than they are
looking for. if this thing haint closed before the next Presidential
Campaign there will be fun rather dier fun though at least that is
my opinion of the matter. I hope old Butler wil get a chance to try
his hand on Richmond it wil be a grand thing if he has luck. well
Jo as I have to get some wood I will close I am well and harty. give
my Love to all the family I would love to see Eme and the Children
write when ever you can nothing more still remain yours as ever

                        Will Leatherwood

                        Fayetteville, West Va.
                        Feb. 11th 1864
Dear Jo
            as I have some spare time I wil write you a few lines to let
you know how I am getting along I am well. I received your letter
on the eighth but could not answer then on the morning of the tenth
went on picket but now I am at your service and wil give you a few
items whether they wil be of any interest to you I wil leave for you
to decide. there is nothing of any grait interest gowing on here. we
had some little excitement the other day about old Granny Scammon he
was captured at red house on the third there wer but few teers shed
in this Brigade I hope he will have a good time of it wel I told you
that I was on Picket and while I was out there was six rebs come in
and gave themselves up I was on the out post so I just sent them to
head quarters under guard they had hardly got out of sight until
there wer three of our Boys come in they had been captured at Chikkamauga and taken to Danville where they broke guard they had worked
there way thrue safe. poor fellows they sufferd a graideel they had
traveled twenty three nights in the cold they came laughing. there
has been a good many come in this way there is no end to the rebs
they come in nearly every day they report the Confederacy gon up
hope it ie so. they are conscripting every thing in this State they
can get. I suppose them fellows think they are safe if they had known
that Old Abe was gowing to make another Reckuisition on them they
would have stayed away longer.
        if any of them Ladies comes around with there subscription just
tell them to put me down on it and I wil pay when I get home. I
would to be there to see the Boys that have reenlisted I rather
think they wil have a hi old time but three years is a big contract
for to get thirty days furlow the opinion of most of the Boys is
that the war wont last long I hope they are rite but I cant see it
that way.

we were paid off the other day but there is no way to send the money
home I have thirty dollars I wish you had the pay agent did not come
this time. I believe I have written all that is nessary for this time
write when ever you can it dont matter to me if they are rong side up
I can read them give my love to Emeand the Babies nothing more
Stil remain your afectionate Brother

                                    Will

                                    Fayetteville, West Va.
                                    Feb. 28th, 64

Wel, Jo,
            Yours of the eighteenth is before me and I hasten to
reply it found me in good helth I was glad to here from home and
here that you and the rest wer all well the River has been closed
for some time so that we did not get any mail but it is open now
the weather has again opened and is pleasent we had some colder
weather than we had the other cold spell. there is but little gowing
on here Old General Crook has command of this Division now we may
look for to do something the comingsummer some think we wil make a
forward move in the Spring but it is uncertin we may and we may not
Such a thing is that we may stay here all Summer although I dont
promis my self any thing of the kind a Soldier cant see his destiny
two hours ahead he cant tell when he wil get orders to go or where
he wil go. I was glad to here that there wer some of the Boys gowing
in yet but I would be like you stay and see the last cat hung. there
are grait inducements for a man to go, one that loves money I thought
some of them you spoke of would be the last ones to go glad they have
they have got as good a rite as any on I would love to be at home
to see the Boys that are on Furlow. I did not know that Hi Easton
was in the Service how I heard he had resigned again. wel I have
but little to write I would be glad to get home to see Tammy and
Willey but have no hopes of it as long as I keepe well and all of
the family it is of but little use for me to come home it would
be a grait pleasure to see all of you. you neede not look for me
any way soon tell Em that I have a present for her which I wil send
some of these days but I must close write soon yours truley

                                    Will Leatherwood

The letter dated Feb. 28, 1864, is the last one from Will in the collection. Battles and Leaders of the Civil War, vol. 4, page 477, says:

"On 9th May (1864) an inferior force commanded by Gen. Albert B. Jenkins engaged the Federals at Cloyd's Mountain, and Jenkins was mortally wounded, his force defeated."

The Confederate leader was not the only one mortally wounded at Cloyd's Mountain. Corporal William H. Leatherwood, Co. E, 91st Ohio Volunteer Infantry, was killed in the battle. To the family back in Adams County this small Federal victory was dearly bought.

Before the last letter above was mailed, Joseph Leatherwood had enrolled in the Union Army (Feb. 29). He was mustered into service March 9, 1864, at Hillsboro, as a private in Co. L of the 2d Ohio Cavalry Volunteers.

The little diary which Joseph carried has an entry on May 15, "Wrote to Brother." A month later, June 14, he wrote, "Received letter from Sister that Brother was dead."

There are not many letters from Joseph Leatherwood himself, though many of his diary entries are about letters received from or written to Emily, his sisters, and his sister-in-law "Tam" Newlon.

The letter dated July 6, 1864, from Knoxville, Tennessee, was written by Tam Newlon's son Enos. It gives some indication of the close family-neighborhood feeling among the Ohio kinfolk.

....

July 6th, 1864
Knoxville, Tenn.

Dear aunt   I take my seat this morning to let you know that I have not forgotten you yet all tho I have not wrote to you since I left home. This leaves me well and I hope it may find you all enjoying the same blessings. I enjoy my self very well heare as well as I did at Covington if not better. We are campt near Fort Sanders east of Knoxville rite in the hot sun not a shade tree in the camp. There is an orcherd clost that we tend very regular about now to find a cool place to sleep.

For some two or three days now we have binllive very hi and at the top of the pot we have been picking blackberries and stewing some and haveing some baked in to pies. An old Negrow woman dose our bakeing and dose it very cheap we had four pies for supper last night and have got enough berries to make as many more.

I want you to write to me and tell me how to direct a letter to uncle Joseph and how he is geting a long since he left Washington. I was sorry to heare of William being killed it made me think of days that are passed, of the many young men that I ust to love to be with that have died and bin killed since this infernal war broke out. I believe that I am the only one left of boys that ust to meet at Mr. Leatherwoods with his two boys and have such good times.

I havent told you about the health of the company. A.R. Fulton, S. Conaulay, O. Garman are all well and the Co. in general has good health. We have plenty to eat such as it is we dont get any beans nor hominy but get good meat, coffee, shugar and crackers and soft bread. Go on guard three times a week and drill two hours a day.

Well I must close you must excuse all mistakes and bad writing. Write soon.

Yours respectfully

E. U. Newlon

Following are a few letters from Joseph Leatherwood.

Camp Cleveland, March the 22nd 1864

Dear Pleasy, after a stroll over the city and to the dock to look at the vessels and geting a look at General Tom Thumb and his wife, Commodore Nut and partner and their minature carriage and ponies, I seat myself in my bunk with the boys all around me laughing and talking and singing, for to try to pen you a few lines to let you know that I am well and in good spirits. I bunk with Denis and Danny, we are all here in quarters together and get a long very well they are all rather civil no drinking at all in our shack there is some card playing that is all. I was out to look at the Lake you can look away out on the water and it looks like a great blue mountain covered with snow it is said that we will leave here tomorrow but it is uncertain about that. I want you to tell Tam that the provision she gave me did me a great service it kept me from suffering and I have some of it yet it was a great favor to me for which I am very mutch oblige to her. As I wrote to you once already and once to Will I shall not write a long leter I hope this may find you all well and in good spirits, keep your heads up recollect us at all times. Talk to the dear little children about pappy tell Tammy and Willy that pappy wants them to be good children and not forget him i hope you got my letter and understood what was in it. The weather is cold this is the first day that it has not snowed since we have ben here. If you want to write to me you can direct to Camp Cleveland and it will folow me.

I dont know of any thing more at present but remain your afectionate Companion til death give my love to all of the friends. Joseph to Emily P. Leatherwood.

Direct to Mr. Joseph Leatherwood, Camp Cleveland Ohio
In care of Capt. Easton, Co. L, 2d OVC, to folow regmt.

Head Quarters 2nd OVC
Camp Stoneman, Sunday April the 24th, 1864

Dear Pleasy, this beautiful day finds me seated on the hights over looking the town of Alexandria and the Potomac it is one of the finest views I ever saw the River dotted over with vessels of all kinds and the hills with camps as far as I can see. If you could just stand by my side one moment you would see sights that would make your blood run cold, thousands of men camped ready to move to the deadly conflict, the long lines of wagons as far as the eye can reach my heart sickens at the sight, war, war, every-thing wears a war like appearance. Near us is a large fort its huge guns frowning angrily out in every direction. O that the time may soon come when there shall be no use for them. We are here in the dismounted camp we struck tents on the 21st, marched to the Railroad, layed out in open field over night the 22nd, started for Washington City got there in the after noon, got out dinner at the soldiers home after which I went to the Capitol and went all over it or nearly so. It is one of the finest things in this world I wish you could see it we stayed all night in the city and until after noon then started for this camp. We marched to the landing, got on boats, came acrost to a point 1½ miles landed and marched to this place which is about 3 or 4 miles from the city. We have not got any arms yet nor cant tell when we will there are thousands of rumors in camp as to what will be done with us, some say we we will stay here for some time some say we will leave soon but none of them know. We will have to be armed and mounted before we take the field. I received a letter from Tam

last Monday the last letter that I have had. I wrote to the girls and thot
to have got an answer before now but it has not come yet. I am well and
harty, can eat anything that I can get, we have had plenty of soft bread
and pork, beef and coffee but now it is hard tack instead of the soft bread.
I have been on Drill every day that there has been Drill since the 7th day
of April I was put at the head of the company and think that I am the best
looking soldier in the Company. I put some rings in the leter to the girls
and shal be sorry if they were miscarried they were for the children, poor
little fellows how I would love to see them. Who that has not left a home
and family can appreciate the comforts of one, how sweet the name of home
sounds in the soldiers ear I hope I shal live to enjoy the comforts of
home. When I started from the camp near Annapolis I gave my old coat to a
poor old Negro and there has just come an order to camp for all who have
citizens clothes to turn them in to the Goverment so I shal have to give
up my pants I cant send them home it wont pay, if there was any old Negro
here I would give them to him. Well her it is all still and nothing else
still and quiet on the Potomac. I hope to hear from you soon you must try
to write to me once a week write about everything you can think of, commence
Sunday & write every day till the letter is done. Well Tammy and Willy,
pappy is well and hopes his little children are well, it pleases pappy to
hear that you think about him and talk about him, he wants you to be good
children mind what mother says to you you must not be saucy to Grandpap
and the girls you must go to school and learn to read and write so you can
rite to pap. You must not fight nor quarrel but be pretty children take
good care of Puss and Jack and old Bird til pappy comes home. I must close
my letter for the present.

Joseph Leatherwood to his Companion
E. P. Leatherwood & Children

Direct to Washington D.C.
Care of Capt. Easton
Co. L, 2d Reg. OVVC
To Follow Regat.

Camp Russell, VA.
February the 6th 1865

Dear Wife, I take the present oportunity to inform you that I am in
pretty good health and hope this may find you enjoying the same blessing.
It seems to me a long time since I heard from any of you and I am geting
impatient for to get some news, there is but little to break the monotony
of camp life save the rumors of peace that come to us. Some put great
confidence in them and even dare to say that there will be no campaign
opened this spring but I cant think so, they will fight. Some of our men
came in this morning from a scout to Mofield' they ran into a rebel conscription camp and captured some prisoners. Scouting picketing and grand
reviews are about all that we have to go through I just came off picket
today and thot that I would drop you a few lines, it was very cold and I
could hardly keep from freezing. Well here comes Sergeant Campbell with
a letter and I must stop and read it is Jan. 29 well I am glad to hear
that you are all well but sorry you are so disapointed about me coming
home. You need not be afraid to fasten the door I hope to get home but
fear that it will be a long time first. I think that Harry was a fool to
tell such stories at home as he did you must not be mutch disapointed if
I dont come. I am thinking of being transfered to Infantry Service thinking that it is about as good as the Cavalry if I can get to a Reg. of my

_____

? Mofield, probably Moorefield, W. Va., some distance west of the Shenandoah Valley where the regiment was located.

choice think that I shall go you can still send on your letters dont wait
for a furlow thinking that I wont get them. You said that you was afraid
the Johneys had got me, they wont get me if I have a horse of any account
without getting some of the rest I have learnt to look out for myself
pretty well. Tell Billy that pappy had a harty laugh for his slay ride
but think he had better not ride with the oxen any more I wish that I was
at home to take him a sleigh ride. It is snowing here today the 7th it
looks as if there was going to be quite a snow things are dull here now,
no pay yet nor no prospect for anyfor some time to come. I am out of writing paper and stamps and if you dont get letters often dont be uneasy for
be sure that I am all right. I wrote to Adlaid some time ago if you see her
ask her if she got the letter I have got some that I have not answered nor
cant for some time. Tell me what has become of Sarah she has not sent me
that letter she told you she would. As there is nothing of interest here I
will close hoping to hear from some of you soon. I am yours till death.

                                        Joseph to Emily P. Leatherwood

                                        Whitehouse Landing, VA.
                                        March the 24th/65

Dear Wife,
            I take the present oportunity to drop you a few lines to let you
know that I am still alive and well and hope this may find you the same. I
received the letters from you one from Tam one each from Rod and Town yesterday evening when I come off picket. I was truly glad to hear from you
that you was all well. As I before stated to you we landed here on the 18th
and are still here after a march of near five hundred miles through rain mud
and fording and swimming deep and rapid rivers drowning men and horses but
through the mercy and providence of God I am safe and sound. I made some incorrece statements in my last fxtkxx as to the distance from here to the
James River I was in a hurry and took flying reports for truth so you will
have to sift my letters. There are many of our men dismounted and I am one
of that number I dont know what they are going to do with us whether they
will send us to the breastworks or remount us but think they will remountuus.
Some of the men think the prospects for peace are very good some of the boys
told me last night that Jef Davis had give it up to Lee and Grant to settle
but that he did long ago so that counts nothing to us. Still I hope that
war will soon close I am tired and want to get home. You spoke of Tap Hite
preaching wish that I could hear him but I hear no preaching nothing but
cursing and swearing there is plenty of that day and night. I would like
for the girls at home to write to me if they can I want you to tell them
for me that I nearly get out of patience some times and think they dont care
for me I shal have but little chance to write for there is going to be a
hard summers work for us the weather here is fine warm and nice but the wind
blows to beat Texas making the sand fly all the time the fruit trees are beginning to bloom. Well Pleasy I some times get in the dumps and feel as if
I dident care how things go then again I think of home and the loved ones
and long to be there I want to see the little hands that marked that letter,
Tammy and Willy I can see but it only makes me feel sad to look at them I
sometimes think of sending the pictures home I cant take very good care of
them here then if the Johneys were to get me they might tare and stamp them
in the ground before my eyes. Often do tears unbidden come when I look at
them and think that I may never see their lively forms or hear their prat-
ling tongues. Remind them of me give my love to all and pray that we may

meet again in this life and finaly in the world to come I remain your loving Companion till death.

                    Joseph to E.P. Leatherwood

            ....

The girls at home, mentioned in Joseph's letters above, were his own sisters. Rod and Town, in the last letter above, were Rodney and Townsend Nichols, brothers of Emily. Adlaid and Sarah were sisters of Emily, while Tan Newlon, another of her sisters, was the one for whom little Tammy was named.   ....

Before the date of the next letter from Joseph, the Confederate army had surrendered. Joseph's regiment was sent to Missouri to await discharge. Perhaps it was largely because of the let-down after the war ended, but it is clear from the last of his letters that Missouri was not Joseph Leatherwood's favorite place ! "No place like home."

            ....

                    Benton Barracks, MO.
                    June the 20th 1865

Dearest Pleasy
            I take my pen once more to write you a few lines just to let you know that I am still alive and in tolerable health and hope this may find you the same. The weather is very warm and makes it very uncomfortable in the Barracks and then we have very bad water and a heap of filth about the back streets so upon the whole it is a very unpleasant place to stay. Then to make the thing still worse about two thirds of the men are drunk most of the time I think that I have saw as disgraceful sights here as ever I saw in my life, last night there was a part of 3 Regiments of infantry came in such a lot of drunken men I never saw. Pleasy I am as near being homesick as ever I was I suppose Major Easton is at home now there is thousands of rumors now in camp there was some horse equipment that came in and now it is for Texas Mexico the plains Rocky Mts and I cant tell where else. I get sick hearing such foolery I would much rather hear something from home for I have not heard from there since I come here and it seems a very long time. I think this the most cramped up place that I ever saw, the place is infested with women pedling bread and vegetables (and some for other purposes) they will ask 5 cents for 5 onions or raddishes or half a dozen cheries they know that such things are tempting to the soldier he gets tired of dry bread coffee and fat meat and some little tastes good to him but he has to pay dear for them. Well Pleas I am writing a heap of letters but I have nothing else to do I went to the Photograph gallery today and engaged some pictures but I know you will scold when you get them but if they dont suit you you must give them away give some of them to the girls anyhow I look tough feel tough and gess I am a little tough I am a Soldier. Some think a soldier is not a man and many of them would make you think so if you could see their acts but I feel the same manly pride that I did at home but I must stop for today.Candle light. Pleasy I got your letter this evening but heard later than that for Jenkins come up this evening I am going to try for a furlow dont know if I shal get it for they say we are going to Springfield, MO. I would like to get my pay first but dont think there is mutch chance now I think I should like to get away from here.

If we dip a mess pan full of water and let it settle there is a half inch of the nastyest mud you ever saw in the bottom of it there is so much confusion

that I must stop. I want you to write often as you can I got a letter from
Rod and Town since I got here. Are you sure that Saminas address is Elwin
that is a singular name nothing more tonight so good night to you.   Good
morning Pleasy this is a nice cool morning and I feel prety well I believe
there is nothing new this morning Jef told me that you had planted the melon
seed but I fear I shal not get to eat the melons this summer, well now I
shal close this poor letter hoping to hear from some of you soon I remain
your loving Companion til death give my love to all even to Jack and Puss.

Joseph. To
Emily P. Leatherwood

You must not get discouraged think I shal get home after a while.

Camp, 2nd OVC
Near Rolla, MO. June 28th/65

Dear Pleasy I take up my pen this morning to inform you that I am still
enjoying good health and hope this may find all of you in the same state
of health. We left the Barracks on the 23 inst. and arrived at Rolla on
the 24th this is the poorest country that I have saw yet the land is very
poor and the people look poorer if there is no better place in Missouri
than this I shal never migrate. The teams are loading our stuff this morning
for Springfield, MO. which is distant about 150 miles this we will have to
foot which will be a hard trip for men not used to walking. I suppose our
business there will be to guard trains to Fort Smith and down in Arkansas I
dont think the duty will be so very hard if the weather dont be to hot it is
extremely hot here. By tracing the map you can see where we are I hope to
get letters from some of you prety often I wrote to Meck before I left Blad-
ensburg and if she got it I fear she has forgot it I wrote to Kate since I
come to St. Louis and hope to hear from her soon I got some pictures and
started them home hope you shal get them if they get through keep of them
for yourself and the children and give the rest to those that may want them
I kept one for Samina if I hear from her I wrote to her but have got no ans.
yet. I want you to tell me how you are off for money Friday is our muster
day then I will have 10 months due me but cant tell when we will be paid I
hear that the goverment is going to stop paying any bounty only to those
that serve out their time now if the thing is going to be worked in that
way dont be surprised if I try to get home before my time is out for if
it is going to fly the track I cant see that I am bound to stick. Now
there is a heap of stories here about our old friend Heistand and the folks
at and about town if there is any thing new just give me a little hint not
so as to knock me down but so that I can understand. Some of you give me the
news generaly I suppose you think that I ought to give you some news but I
dont know a thing we dont get a paper and if we do there is little or nothing
in it tell Pap when I get to Springfield I will try and write him a short
letter if I can. Now I want you to write as often as you can once in 10 days
any how three or four of you certainly can do that hoping to hear soon I
will close. Give my love to all I remain as ever your faithful and loving
companion till death. Farewell for the present.

Jos. to Emily P. Leatherwood

I wrote a letter to Leah some time ago and have not heard from it yet.
Direct your letters to Springfield, MO.

****

Kate and Leah, mentioned above, were two of Joseph's sisters; Meck was his
sister America. Samina (Nichols) Carpenter was one of Emily's sisters, the
one who lived past age 100.

From Emily to Joseph, evidently written in 1865.

                                                    May the 9th
Well Joseph
            I seat my self this plesant sabbeth morning to informe you
that we are all well at present and hope this may find you the same. I
recived your leter you sent while at Rolla allso the one with the pictures
eleven of them we was much pleased with them Tammy knew them Willey dident
know them he was quite outdun when I told him (w)ho it was to think he
didenot know them. I gave each of youre sisters one of them am going to
give Rodnah and Tam one if they want sum the rest I will ceap awhile send
that one on to Samina as you are moving you may miss hur. Hur and Gip rote
to me last fall to send them youre address I never sent it til you went to
MO. You sed you wanted me to giv you the news I hant got eny to giv I hant
bin to town anley once in awhile to the store and to meeting once intm to
or three weeks dont here much. As for our old friend Heistad I hant herd
eny thing new I wood like fore you to give me a hint of what you herd out
thare he has bin vary accomidating to me sence you left if I want eny thing
and hant got the money I can get it from Heistand without. I have 1 hundred
dolers ih the hous I want to keep if I can I lent Enos 20 dolers I will get
as soon as he is pade he has one years pay coming to him I never got but ten
dolers from the co. I got an order fore ten more in May but thare hant eny
money come in sence. Goods has bin so hi sence you went away it tuck a heap
to cloath us I make as litel do as I can I wood like to save a litel if I
can. I will have three hogs to faten this fall will have corn to try to
faten them Pap has a fine prospect fore corne. You sed that you herd that
the government was going to yank the men out of the bounty the way I herd
it thay will get according to the time thay stay I think that will be fare
I want you to come home as soon as you can but never run of, tell them you
are sick or that youre leg hurts and you can get a discarge solgers are coming home all the time the 1st O V H (?) has got home all onley the new recruts and the boys that is at Covington. Jos Heistands boys is at camp
denison I hope thare will not be so meney solgers wimen about as has bin
and the people will have somethin else to talk about if they ever sed any
thing about me I dont know it I dont care how much thay talk if thay tell
the truth.
            After a harty diner and a fine rain I hasten to close my pore
leter my pen is worne out and I cant think to get one you must take care of
youre self Anna ses she is going to kiss papey when he comes. Nothing more
but remain yure loving companion till death farewell.

                                        E.P.L. to Joseph Leatherwood

Since I finished my leter Sara Kisling came and brot youre coat and blanket
the things was in the pocket.

                 ....

     It seems unlikely that Emily rated "A" in spelling, though she did
have plenty of small home news to tell.

Letter from Joseph Leatherwood to his son Will, after a trip to Ohio

On letterhead: OFFICE OF JOS. LEATHERWOOD, JUSTICE OF THE PEACE, Valley Township, Morris County, Kansas

Dunlap, Kansas, Nov. 10, 1891

Dear Will,

I shal try to write you a few lines to let you know how we are getting along but first - I had about made up my mind to pay you a visit this fall, but the death of your grandpap called me to Ohio. So I had to give up a trip westward, then my trip East and the worry and work that I had to do there nearly killed me off. I undertook to settle up the little estate and thought to get it all done before I come home but as the last of the Garman notes is not due until next April I could not get through. So I will have to go back again. The business is in an unsatisfactory shape, the three hundred dollars paid on the old place last spring is lost. I failed to get any account of it and I am forced to believe that Bruce Hammon stole it after your Grandpap died, the circumstances all seem to point in that direction. Now he comes in with a bill of one hundred and fifty dollars for keeping the old man for three months and three days, and he was not helpless only a few days before he died. I dont know whether I can get through without a law suit or not. Old Nat Smith has also acted the dog, I doubt if I get enough out of it to get the old man a monument to mark his grave. I shal not do all of my work at my own expense.

There was a letter from you when I got home, came soon after I left home and I ought to have answered sooner but I have had so much to do and suffered so much with my limbs that I think you will excuse me. Sam and Mace were both gone when I come home and it looked quite lonesome. Soon as I could I put the boys to husking corn and helped them a little, and we have the little field across the creek all in and a little of the other. It is fine weather to get in corn, but I had the boys start to school this morning, will try to hire someone to husk corn. Our corn is pretty fair, weather very dry, hard on the young wheat. It was so dry we did not sow but very little this fall. Our potato crop is pretty good, had thirty or thirty-five bushels, they are selling for 50 cts. per bu. We will have apples enough to do us if they keep good.

Crops in Ohio are fine this year, they had a good season. Hi Easton said he did not see why I did not buy me a horse and cart so I could travel about and stay there a year. Morhead says, You can't work so stay here. The people have treated me royally, waited on me as though I was some great man. Poor Ot Byrd, I did not get to see him, he died last summer. Ag Garman is teaching at old Oakland this winter, the old school-house is in a very dilapidated condition. I tell you everything looked old in that country. Jake Tener's family is nearly all scattered and Jake is pretty nearly broke up. Aunt Tam lives with Sarah in the Springs, I tried to persuade her to come home with me but she cant leave the old place. Enos is still working for Leighton and cussing democrats. Will Auckerman still lives down near the Grove, they have a pretty hard time of it. Jake has enlisted in the regular army, he was away from home at work when he enlisted, dont know why he did it. He is at Ft. Thomas near Covington, Ky. Aaron worked for Will Cannon this year for $13.00 per month.

Now I will get back home. The same darned old crew still hold out in Dunlap, just sit around and howl calamity and hard times. Curse the people's party anyhow, but we knocked the wind out of them this fall.

J.R. has flopped over to the new party and is a full fledged reb and anarchist. To hades with the whole infernal crew. Tam was at home while I was gone, the boys have heard from her since. They get letters I dont know what is in them. I would like you to write if Elliott is still near you. Guess I will come out and catch some of them bears that steal Katy's black berries. And Mister Lonzo and Jim, I can just throw you down and I will sure. Here is the boys home from school and I am tired and must quit, with love to all and hoping to hear from you soon I am ever your loving

                                        Pap.

Part IV

Unit Histories of the
Second Ohio Cavalry
Twenty-Fourth Ohio Infantry
Ninety-First Ohio Infantry

Sgt. George B. Kennedy and an unidentified Comrade
Company D, 2nd OVC
Courtesy of and Copyright © L.M. Strayer Collection

Unit Histories

The unit histories cover only those periods in which each one of these men served. The Second Ohio Cavalry served all over the South through different detachments. Joseph D. Leatherwood was discharged a Sergeant on October 12, 1865, at Benton Barracks (Saint Louis), Missouri. Sergeant Samuel Leatherwood served the shortest amount of time losing his life on October 8, 1861, only months into the War of the Rebellion. He was killed at Cheat Mountain Summit in present day West Virginia. Samuel served with the 24th Ohio Volunteer Infantry, one of the north's most celebrated units having fought from the mountains of West Virginia, Shiloh, Corinth, Athens, Murfreesborough, Chickamauga and Chattanooga to list the highlights of the places and battles they fought. Corporal William Leatherwood served the longest. He served with the 91st Regiment Ohio Volunteer Infantry. He died May 9, 1864, at Cloyd's Mountain, West Virginia. The 91st Regiment fought throughout the West Virginia and Western Virginia Theatre of operations.

A History of the Second Ohio Cavalry
Joseph D. Leatherwood, Sergeant

Record of Events for the Second Ohio Cavalry

GENERAL NOTATION: War Department, Adjutant-Generals Office, Washington, October 15, 1877. The regiment was ordered to proceed from Saint Louis, Missouri to Springfield, Missouri by railroad, Special Orders No. 166, Department of the Missouri, June 21, 1865.

DETACHMENT: Stationed at Cleveland, Ohio, September-October 1863. September 28, 1863 – this party was ordered to Ohio from the field to take charge to drafted men to be assigned to the regiment. As the draft was avoided in Ohio by volunteering, no men were assigned and by orders of General [Egbert Ludovicus] Viele, commanding Draft Rendezvous, the party become a recruiting party.

DETACHMENT: Stationed at Knoxville, Tennessee, March – April 1864. This detachment is composed of men belonging to Company D, Second Ohio Volunteer Cavalry, who did not reenlist as veterans. They compose the escort at Headquarters of Brigadier-General [Samuel Powhatan] Carter, Provost Marshal General of East Tennessee, Knoxville, Tennessee. Signed W.H. Thomas, Captain and Assistant Adjust-General.

DETACHMENT: Stationed at Fort Ripley, Minnesota, January-February 1865. November 10, 1864. Attached to Captain Boyd's command by orders of Major [John] M. Thompson, commanding post, Special Orders No. 145. Private Brookins sent from Camp Chase, Ohio to Columbus, Ohio and forwarded to headquarters, Northwestern District.

FIELD AND STAFF: Stationed at Camp Wade, October 10, 1861. October 10 – Muster-in roll of the field and staff officers in the Second Cavalry Regiment of Ohio Volunteers commanded by Colonel Charles Doubleday, called into the service of he United States by the President, thereof, under th Act of Congress approved July 22, 1861, From October 10, 1861 (date of this muster) from the term of three years, unless sooner discharged. Signed: James P. [Wilson] Neill, First Lieutenant, Eighteenth Infantry, Mustering Officer.

Company L Military Operations: Includes only the period of service of Joseph D. Leatherwood March 1864 – June 1865.

From	To	Comments
March 1864		Camp Cleveland, Ohio
January 1864	April 1864	Stationed at Camp Stoneman, District of Columbia
January 7, 1864	January 30, 1864	Detachment: Left Mossy Creek, East Tennessee per Special Order No. 8 dated Headquarters, Cavalry Corps, Department of Ohio. Arrived at Camp Chase, Ohio on January 30.
February 16, 1864	March 17, 1864	Furloughed from thence for thirty days. Returned from furlough. Rendezvoused at Cleveland, Ohio March 17.
March 24, 1864	March 28, 1864	Left Cleveland. Arrived Annapolis, Maryland March 28.
April 22, 1864	April 23, 1864	Left Annapolis, Maryland. Arrived at Camp Stoneman, District Columbia April 23.
May 1864	June 1864	Stationed at Lighthouse Point, Virginia
May 1, 1864	May 3, 1864	The company, with the regiment, left Washington, District of Columbia and marched to Warrenton Junction, where it joined the Ninth Army Corps May 3.
May 4, 1864		Crossed the Rapidan [River] and were place on picket at the extreme right of the Army.
May 7, 1864	May 8, 1864	Had slight skirmish. No loss in the company.
May 9, 1864	May 12, 1864	Were on the march.
May 15, 1864		Had slight skirmish at Piney Branch Church. Sustained no loss in the company.
May 28, 1864		Joined the Cavalry Crops.
May 31, 1864	June 1, 1864	Had a severe skirmish at Hanover Court-House and Ashland, Virginia. Lost two officers and two men wounded and one man missing.
June 17, 1864		Had a skirmish at White Oak Swamp. One man missing.
June 28, 1864	June 29, 1864	Had a severe cavalry fight at Stony Creek and Reams' Station, Virginia. Lost one man killed, four wounded and seven missing.
July 1864	August 1864	Stationed at Berryville, Virginia. Joseph D. Leatherwood was detached and in Knoxville, Tennessee in July 1864.
September 1864	October 1864	Stationed at Cedar Creek, Virginia.
November 1864	December 1864	Stationed at Camp Russell, Virginia.
January 1865	February 1865	Stationed in the field, Virginia.
April 30, 1865		Stationed in the field, Virginia.
May 1865	June 1865	Stationed at Big Piney River, Missouri.
October 12, 1865		Joseph D. Leatherwood discharged from the unit at Benton Barracks, Missouri (Saint Louis).

A History of the 24th Regiment, Ohio Volunteer Infantry
Samuel Leatherwood, Sergeant

Record of Events for Twenty-fourth Ohio Infantry, May 1862-June 1864. Muster-in roll of the field and staff officers, twenty-fourth regiment of Ohio Volunteers, commanded by Colonel Jacob Ammen, called into service of the United States by the President from June 18, 1861 (date of this muster) for the term of three years, unless sooner discharged.

Company E Military Operations: Includes only the period of time covering the service of Samuel Leatherwood.

From	To	Comments
May 29, 1861		Muster-in roll of the Captain Samuel B. Jackson, Company E into the twenty-fourth regiment of Ohio Volunteers, commanded by Colonel E.P. Scammon, called into service of the United States by the President from May 29, 1861 (date of this muster) for the term of three years, unless sooner discharged.
June 12, 1861		Stationed at Camp Jackson
May 29, 1861	August 31, 1861	Stationed at Cheat Mountain Summit, [West] Virginia
September 1861	October 1861	Stationed at Cheat Mountain Summit, [West], Virginia.
October 8, 1861		Samuel Leatherwood lost his life at Cheat Mountain
1861	1864	Twenty-fourth Regiment of Ohio Volunteers fought at some of the Civil Wars pivotal battles: Shiloh, Corinth, Murfreesborough, Chickamauga and Chattanooga.
June 17, 1864		Muster-out

A History of the 91st Regiment, Ohio Volunteer Infantry
William Hamilton Leatherwood, Corporal

Organized in August, 1862, under Colonel John A. Turley, it served along the Ohio River until September, when it moved to West Virginia, and operated in the Kanawha Valley and further east during the winter and spring of 1862-63. In July, 1863, it joined the forces in pursuit of Morgan in Ohio, but soon returned to West Virginia, where it passed its second winter. In May, 1864, it made a successful raid up New River under General Crook, marching over 200 miles over mountains and through wild forests. In June the Regiment joined Hunter's march upon Lynchburg, and near that place made a gallant charge, capturing two pieces of artillery. It returned with the army in its disastrous retrograde movement, the men completely worn out and after only nine days rest moved by rail to Martinsburg, where it served against Early's army. It fought up and down the Shenandoah Valley all the summer, fighting at Winchester, Fisher's Hill and Opequan; at the latter place the 91st lost heavily, having charged the Rebels, posted behind a stone wall, but lifted them out of their position with the bayonet. The Regiment served in this vicinity until the close of the war and was mustered out June 24, 1865.

From Dyer's Compendium

91st Regiment Infantry.

Organized at Camp Ironton, Ohio, August 26, 1862. Moved to Ironton, Ohio, August 26-September 3, thence to Guyandotte, Va., September 4. Mustered into United States service September 5. Ordered to Maysville, Ky., September 15. Orders changed to Point Pleasant, W. Va. Attached to District of the Kanawha, W. Va., Dept. of the Ohio, to March. 1863. 2nd Brigade, 3rd Division, 8th Army Corps, Middle Dept., to June, 1863. 2nd Brigade, Scammon's Division, Dept, of West Virginia, to December, 1863. 2nd Brigade. 3rd Division, Dept. West Virginia, to April, 1864. 2nd Brigade, 2nd Infantry Division, West Virginia, to January, 1865. 1st Brigade, 3rd Division, West Virginia, to April, 1865. 1st Brigade, 4th Provisional Division, West Virginia, to June, 1865.

REGIMENT SERVICE.--Duty at Point Pleasant, Va., till September 26. 1862. Raid up the Kanawha to Buffalo September 26-28. Action at Buffalo September 27. Advance to Gauley Bridge, Falls of the Great Kanawha, October 20-November 3, thence moved to Fayetteville November 8, and duty there till April, 1863. Advance to Summerville April. Duty at Summerville and Fayetteville till May, 1864. Pursuit of Morgan July 20-31, 1863. Expedition from Charleston to Lewisburg November 3-13. Scammon's demonstration from the Kanawha Valley December 8-21. Big Sewell and Meadow Bluff December 11. Lewisburg and Greenbrier River December 12. Crook's Expedition to Dublin Depot and New River Bridge, Virginia & Tennessee Railroad, May 2-19, 1864. Cloyd's Mountain May 9. New River Bridge and Newbern Bridge May 10. March to join Hunter at Staunton May 31-June 4. Piedmont June 5. Hunter's Raid to Lynchburg June 10-July 1. Diamond Hill June 17. Lynchburg June 17-18. Buford's Gap June 20. Salem June 21. Moved to the Shenandoah Valley July 8, and reached Martinsburg July 15. Stevenson's Depot July 20. Battle of Winchester, Kernstown, July 24. Martinsburg July 25. Sheridan's Shenandoah Valley Campaign August 7-November 28. Near Charlestown August 24. Halltown August 24. Near Charlestown August 26. Halltown August 26. Wormley's Gap August 29. Berryville September 3. Battle of Opequan, Winchester, September 19. Fisher's Hill September 22. Battle of Cedar Creek October 19, Kablestown November 18. Guarding Railroad Bridge at Opequan till December 20. Ordered to Martinsburg December 30, and duty Guarding Railroad Bridge at Opequan till December 20. Ordered to Martinsburg December 30, and duty there till March 17, 1865. Moved to Cumberland, Md., March 17, thence to Winchester April 5, and duty there till June 2. At Cumberland, Md., till June 24.

Killed in Action: The following members of Company E died in service: Captain Samuel E. Clark killed in the battle of Cloyd's Mountain, Va. and William A. Leatherwood killed in the battle of Cloyd's Mountain, Va.

Mustered out June 24, 1865. Regiment lost during service 3 Officers and 60 Enlisted men killed and mortally wounded and 3 Officers and 87 Enlisted men by disease. Total 153.

Companies by County

Company A Gallia County	Company B Gallia County
Company C Scioto County	Company D Hamilton County and Mix
Company E Adams County	Company F Scioto County
Company G Pike County	Company H Lawrence and Pike Counties
Company I Adams County	Company K Jackson County

Station not stated, not dated. Muster-in roll of the field and staff officers, Ninety-first regiment of Ohio Volunteers, commanded by Colonel John (Alexander) Turley, called into service of the United States by the President from September 7, 1862 (date of this muster) for the term of three years, unless sooner discharged. Signed: S. Beall, Captain, United States Army, Mustering Officer.

Company E Military Operations: Muster-in roll of the Captain Samuel E. Clark's Compay E into the Ninety-first regiment of Ohio Volunteers, commanded by Colonel John (Alexander) Turley, called into service of the United States by the President from September 7, 1862 (date of this muster) for the term of three years, unless sooner discharged. Signed: S. Beall, Captain, United State Army, Mustering Officer.

From	To	Comments
September 7, 1862	October 31, 1862	Station status not stated
November 1862	February 1863	Stationed at Fayetteville, [West] Virginia
April 10, 1863		Stationed at Kanawha Falls, [West] Virginia

March 1863	April 1863	Stationed at Camp Reynolds, [West] Virginia
May 1863	June 1863	Stationed at Gauley Bridge, [West] Virginia
July 1863	August 1863	Stationed at Fayette Court House, West Virginia
September 1863	April 1864	Stationed at Fayetteville, West Virginia
May 1864	June 1864	Stationed at Camp Piatt, West Virginia: This company marched about 670 miles since may 3, 1864, having moved from Fayetteville on that date toward Cloyd's Mountain near Dublin Depot, Virginia, where it was engaged losing two killed, five wounded and one missing.
May 19, 1864		Returned to Meadow Bluff
May 31, 1864		Again moved from Meadow Bluff marching via Staunton and Liberty to Lynchburg was engaged in three skirmishes on Cow Pasture River, Virginia losing one man.

Part V

Post War Letters of
Joseph D. Leatherwood

Letter from Joseph Leatherwood
to his son Will, after a trip to Ohio

On letterhead:
OFFICE OF JOS. LEATHERWOOD,
JUSTICE OF THE PEACE,
Valley Township, Morris County, Kansas
 Dunlap, Kansas, Nov. 10, 1891

Dear Will,

I shal try to write you a few lines to let you know how we are getting along but first - I had about made up My mind to pay you a visit this fall, but the death of your grandpap called me to Ohio. So I had to give up a trip westward, then my trip East and the worry and work that I had to do there nearly killed me off. I undertook to settle up the little estate and thought to get it all done before I came home but as the last of the Garman notes is not due until next April I could not get through. So I will have to go back agin. The business is in an unsatisfactory shape, the three hundred dollars paid on the old place last spring is lost. I failed to get any account of it and I am forced to believe that Bruce Hammon stole it after your Grandpap died, the circumstances all seem to point in that direction. Now he comes in with a bill of one hundred and fifty dollars for keeping the old man for three months and three days, and he was not helpless only a few days before he died. I don't know whether I can get through without a law suit or not. Old Nat Smith has also acted the dog, I doubt if I get enough out of it to get the old man a monument to mark his grave. I shal not do all of my work at my own expense.

There was a letter from you when I got home, came soon after I left home and I ought to have answered sooner but I have had so much to do and suffered so much with my limbs that I think you will excuse me. Sam and Mace were both gone when I come home and it looked quite lonesome. Soon as I could I put the boys to husking corn and helped them a little, and we had the little field across the creek all in and a little of the other. It is fine weather to get in corn, but I had the boys start to school this morning, will try to hire someone to husk corn. Our corn is pretty fair, weather very dry, hard on the young wheat. It was so dry we did not sow but very little this fall. Our potato crop is pretty good, had thirty or thirty-five bushels, they are selling for 50 cts. per bu. We will have apples enough to do us if they keep good.

Crops in Ohio are fine this year, they had a good season. Hi Easton said he did not see why I did not buy me a horse and cart so I could travel about and stay there a year. Morhead says, you can't work so stay here. The people have treated me royally, waited on me as though I was some great man. Poor Ol Byrd, I did not get to see him, he died last sumner. Ag Garman is teaching at old Oakland this winter, the old school-house is in a very dilapidated condition. I tell you everything looked old in that country. Jake Teener's family is nearly all scattered and Jake is pretty nearly broke up. Aunt Tam lives with Sarah in the Springs, I tried to persuade her to come home with me but she cant leave the old place. Enos is still working for Leighton and cussing democrats. Will Auckerman still lives down near the Grove, they have a pretty hard time of it. Jake has enlisted in the regular army, he was away from home at work when he enlisted, dont know why he did it. He is at Ft. Thomas near Covington, Ky. Aaron worked for Will Cannon this year for $13.00 per month.

Now I will get back home. The same darned old crew still hold out in Dunlap, just sit around and howl calamity and hard times. Curse the people's party anyhow, but we knocked the wind out of them this fall. J.R. has flopped over to the new party and is a full fledged reb and anarchist. To hades with the whole infernal crew. Tam was at home while I was gone, the boys have heard from her since. They get letters I dont know what is in them. I would like you to write if Elliott is still near you. Guess I will come out and catch some of them bears that steal Katy's black berries. And Mister Lonso and Jim, I can just throw you down and I will sure. Here is the boys home from school and I am tired and must quit, with love to all and hoping to hear from you soon I am ever your loving.

Pap

Letter from William Leatherwood to Joseph Leatherwood

Dodge City, Kansas
April 2nd, 1892

Joseph Leatherwood, esq.
Dunlap, Kansas

Dear Sir:

Yours of the 27th pen to hand and replying will say that for a long time I believed that I was the only Leatherwood who had ventured across that Great Father of Waters. On coming to Dodge City I learned my mistake when the postmaster handed me a letter which was addressed to Luther M. Leatherwood. This letter was posted at a little cattle town in western Texas.

When the State Forestry was established at Dodge City in the Spring of 1887, the manager informed me that a gentlemen of the name worked for the Emporia Nursery, but he could not give me his first name or initials. While I was in Russell last summer Professor Gordon informed me that a young man whose name was Leatherwood attended the State Normal.

In regard to my ancestors I will say that Henry J. L. was not my father and I never heard the man until I receive your letter.

To trace my genealogy for two hundred years is not a very difficult task, and yet it may throw very little light on the point in question as I can trace it in the direct line only.

John Leatherwood emigrated from Dovershire in England in the Spring of 1680 and located in what in now Carroll Co. Md. The following Autumn he marred Miss Mollie Kitteu, a half Indian girl. To this union were born nine children two of whom were boys and seven girls. John and Saumel were the names of these two boys. I am not certain but think that Samuel was the youngest of the family, and was born in 1699. On reaching his majority John went to North Carolina and none of the old people among those in Maryland knew anything of him or his descendants afterwards, but while I was in Missouri I learned from Captain Reider and Mr. Luce Weaver that in a certain part of N.C. the name is common today.

Samuel Letherwood remained in Maryland and occupied the old homestead during his life. He married Hannah Buchkingham of English descent and they were blessed with a family of nine children seven girls and two boys.

I can not account for all the marriages of the sisters of Samuel Leatherwood but think that two of them married Buckinghams, brothers of Samuel's wife. Among other names who became connected with the family were Shipley, Frazier, Gorsuch. Samuel's two boys were John and Zachariah the latter of whom emigrated to Ohio in early day. And I know only of one son Aaron who was a Methodist preacher. I had been informed of this fact by two great aunts. And since coming here I learned that it was a fact. A Mrs. Boyd who resides here say she was christened by him when a child and married by him when she was a Boyd who resides here say she was christened by him when a child and married by him when she was a woman. When my brother was in Wheeling, W.Va. he met two young men who were the sons of Aaron L. There was also a daughter.

John L. remained in Maryland. He was a soldier in the War of 1812 and was married three times. To the first marriage was born two daughters one of whom is still living in Md. And the other one died at Genesis. … about three years ago, his second marriage was with a Miss Gilliss who inherited from her father quite an estate. To this union was born a son and daughter. His third marriage was with Elizabeth Cushon of Irish descent. Three girls and one boy were raised of those born to this union. The boys were named Hanson and Jesse both of whom lived and died in Md. To each family were born the accustomed nine children but four in Hanson's and Jesse families were boys. The whole family were raised in the case of my uncle, but two in my father's family were raised. Jesse was my father. I have a brother in Md. also a teacher. It seems that the highest ambition of the old L's was to raise wheat and corn enough to bread the family and feed the hogs for meat and feed the horses while raising another crop. My grandfather, John L. with properity on his second marriage, became intemperate and indulged in the common sport among men of that class there of fighting simply to see which was the better man. Much of his time was spent in this way to the neglect of the education of his children.

There were some Leatherwoods in Baltimore whose origin I do not know. Two boys and a girl. John was a blacksmith, forman in the Catonsville Horse R.R. shops and his brother was a coach trimmer. The daughter was married to an engineer on the B. & P. R.R. Hanson's sons are all in the east. His oldest daughter is in Denver. Elizabeth, Hanson's sister, married a man by the name of Doty who was superintendent of the Gas Works in Columbus from 1849 to 1875 or 6.

You can tell to which of these lines you belong if to any. It is highly important that the complete line be traced. It is possible that subsequent emigrations brought others of the name came to American after John came in 1680 who located at other places.

Let me hear from you again in this matter telling me what you have asked me, that is, who you are and what you are trying to do in breezy Kansas.

Yours Truly,

William Leatherwood

Dodge City, Kans.
April 2d 1892.

Joseph Leatherwood Esq,
Dunlap.
Kans.

Dear Sir:-
Yours of the 27th ult. to hand
and replying will say that for a long
time I believed that I was the only
Leatherwood who had ventured across the
Great Father of Waters. On coming to
Dodge City I learned my mistake when
the postmaster handed me a letter which
was addressed to Luther M. Leatherwood.
This letter was postmarked at a little cattle
town in western Texas.
When the State Forestry was established at
Dodge City in the spring of 1887 the
manager informed me that a gentleman
of the name worked for the Emporia
Nursery, but he could not give me his
first name or initials

While I was at Russell last summer
Prof Gordon informed me that a young
man whose name was Leatherwood attended
the State Normal.

In regard to my ancestors I will say that
Henry J. L. was not my father and I never heard
of the man until I received your letter.

To trace my genealogy for two hundred years
is no very difficult task, and yet it may
throw very little light on the point in
question as I can trace it in the direct line
only.

John Leatherwood emigrated from Dovershire in
England in the spring of 1680 and located in
what is now Carroll Co. Md. the following autumn.
He married Miss Mollie Kitlew, a half Indian
girl. To this union were born nine children
two of whom were boys and seven girls.
John and Samuel were the names of these
two boys. I am not certain but think that
Samuel was the youngest of the family, and
was born in 1699. On reaching his majority
John went to North Carolina and none of the old
people among those in Md. knew any thing

of him or his descendants afterwards, but while I was in Missouri I learned from Capt Reider and Mr Luce Weaver that in a certain part of NC the name is common to-day.

Samuel L remained in Md and occupied the old homestead during his life. He married Hannah Buckingham of English descent and they were blessed with a family of nine children, seven girls and two boys.

I cannot not account for all the marriages of the sisters of Samuel L but think that two of them married Buckinghams, one of Samuel's wife. Among other names who become connected with the family were Shipley, Frazier, Gorsuch &c. Saml's two boys were John and Zachariah the latter of whom emigrated to Ohio in early day. and I know only of one son Aaron who was a Methodist preacher. I had been informed of this fact by two great aunts. and since Coming here I learned that it was a fact. A Mrs Boyd who resides here says she was christened by him when a child and married by him when she was a woman. When My brother was in Wheeling, W Va he met two young men who were the sons of Aaron L. There was also a daughter.

John L. remained in Md. He was a soldier in the war of 1812. and was married three times. To the first marriage was born two daughters one of whom is still living in Md. and the other one died at Genesis. Ill about three years ago. His second marriage was with a Miss Gilliss who inherited from her father quite an estate. To this union was born a son and daughter. His third marriage was with Elizabeth Cushin of Irish descent. Three girls and one boy were raised of those born to this union. The boys were named Hanson and Jesse both of whom lived and died in Md. To each family were born the accustomed nine children but four in Hanson's and Jessi's families were boys. The whole family were raised in the case of my Uncle, but two in my father's family were raised. Jesse was my father. I have a brother in Md also a teacher. It seems that the highest ~~ambition~~ of the old L's was to raise wheat and corn enough to bread the family and feed the hogs for meat and feed the horses while raising another crop. My grandfather John L. with prosperity on his second marriage, became intemperate and indulged in the common sport among men of that class there, of fighting simply to see which was the better man. Much of his time was spent in this way to the neglect of the education of his children.

There were some Leatherwoods in Baltimore whose origin I do not know. Two boys and a girl. John was a blacksmith, foreman in the Catonsville Horse RR shops, and his brother was a coach trimmer. The daughter was married to an Engineer on the B&O RR. Hanson's sons are all in the east. His oldest daughter is in Denver. Elizabeth, Hanson's sister, married a man by the name of Doty who was Supt. of the Gas Works in Columbus from 1849 to 1875 or 6.

You can tell which of these lines you belong if to any. It is highly important that the complete line be traced. It is possible that subsequent emigrations brought others of the name _____ to America after John came in 1680 and located at other places.

Let me hear from you again in this matter telling me what you have asked me, that is, who you are and what you are trying to do in breezy Kansas.

Yours truly.

Wm Leatherwood

Part VI

A Genealogy Report for
Joseph D. Leatherwood
and
Emily Pleasant Nichols

Timeline Report for Joseph D. Leatherwood

Yr/Age	Event	Date/Place/Description
1831	Birth	23 Dec 1831 Sinking Springs (Highland), Ohio
1833 1	Birth (Spouse) Emily Pleasant Nichols	13 Jan 1833 Loudoun County, Virginia
1835 3	Birth (Sister) Leah Elizabeth "Betsy" Leatherwood	22 Nov 1835 Locust Grove (Adams), Ohio
1838 6	Birth (Brother) Samuel Leatherwood	Abt. 1838 Locust Grove (Adams), Ohio
1839 7	Birth (Brother) William Hamilton Leatherwood	07 Sep 1839 Locust Grove (Adams), Ohio
1841 9	Birth (Sister) Nancy Catherine "Kate" Leatherwood	Abt. 1841 Locust Grove (Adams), Ohio
1844 12	Birth (Sister) America Belle "Meek" Leatherwood	17 Feb 1844 Locust Grove (Adams), Ohio
1846 14	Birth (Sister) Mary Elizabeth Leatherwood	23 Mar 1846 Locust Grove (Adams), Ohio
1848 16	Birth (Sister) Martha J. "Jennie" Leatherwood	Aug 1848 Adams County, Ohio
1850 18	Residence	1850 Franklin (Adams), Ohio; Age: 18
1856 24	Marriage Emily Pleasant Nichols	09 Oct 1856 Adams County, Ohio
1858 26	Birth (Daughter) Tamzen Jane "Tammie" Leatherwood	01 Feb 1858 Sinking Springs (Highland), Ohio
1858 26	Death (Mother) Elizabeth Hamilton	03 May 1858 Locust Grove (Adams), Ohio; Age: 45
1859 27	Birth (Son) William R. "Willy" Leatherwood	07 Jun 1859 Sinking Springs (Highland), Ohio
1860 28	Residence	1860 Brush Creek (Highland), Ohio
1860 28	Marriage (Sister) Leah Elizabeth "Betsy" Leatherwood	Aft. 27 Jul 1860 Adams County, Ohio; It is believed Leah married Theodore Collins during 1860 but after the date cited. The marriage occurred soon after the 1860 census, probably August or

		September 1860, based on the birth of their first child, John W. Collins, on 19 July 1861.
1861 29	Birth (Daughter) Hannah Elizabeth Leatherwood	11 Feb 1861 Sinking Springs (Highland), Ohio
1861 29	Death (Brother) Samuel Leatherwood	08 Oct 1861 Cheat Mountain, Virginia; Sergeant Samuel Leatherwood died in a camp hospital from Typhoid fever.
1862 30	Death (Daughter) Hannah Elizabeth Leatherwood	06 Mar 1862 Sinking Spring (Highland), Ohio
1862 30	Birth (Daughter) Anna M. Leatherwood	15 Dec 1862 Sinking Springs (Highland), Ohio
1863 31	Residence	01 Jul 1863 Franklin (Adams), Ohio; Marital Status: Married
1864 32	Military Regiment	1864 Second Ohio Cavalry
1864 32	Military Service	29 Feb 1864 Ohio; March 9, 1864 to October 12, 1865
1864 32	Military Branch	09 Mar 1864 Ohio; Union Army: 2nd Regiment, Ohio Cavalry, Company L, Rank-in: private, rank-out: Sergeant.
1864 32	Death (Brother) William Hamilton Leatherwood	09 May 1864 Cloyd's Mountain, Virginia
1865 33	Military Rank	12 Oct 1865 Benton Barracks (St. Louis), Missouri; ranked out as Sergeant
1866 34	Birth (Son) Samuel Townsend Leatherwood	09 Sep 1866 Sinking Springs (Highland), Ohio
1867 35	Marriage (Sister) Nancy Catherine "Kate" Leatherwood	Abt. 1867 Adams County, Ohio
1869 37	Birth (Son) Macy Edwin Leatherwood	16 Sep 1869 Sinking Springs (Highland), Ohio
1872 40	Birth (Son) Roscoe Aaron Leatherwood	09 Feb 1872 Sinking Springs (Highland), Ohio
1874 42	Birth (Son) Joseph Harlan Leatherwood	20 May 1874 Sinking Springs (Highland), Ohio
1880 48	Residence	1880 Dunlap (Morris), Kansas
1880	Residence	1880

48		Valley (Morris), Kansas; Age: 48; Marital Status: Married; Relation to Head of House: Self
1882 50	Death (Spouse) Emily Pleasant Nichols	13 Sep 1882 Dunlap (Morris), Kansas
1882 50	Marriage (Son) William R. "Willy" Leatherwood	21 Dec 1882 Dunlap (Morris), Kansas
1885 53	Residence	01 Mar 1885 Valley (Morris), Kansas; Marital Status: Married
1885 53	Property	13 Jul 1885 Morris County, Kansas; Purchased property.
1887 55	Death (Daughter) Anna M. Leatherwood	30 Mar 1887 Ohio; Age: 24
1889 57	Residence	1889 Dunlap (Morris), Kansas
1891 59	Marriage (Daughter) Tamzen Jane "Tammie" Leatherwood	04 Jun 1891 Dunlap (Morris), Kansas
1891 59	Death (Father) Aaron Leatherwood	21 Jul 1891 Locust Grove (Adams), Ohio; Age: 84
1892 60	Residence	1892 Dunlop (Morris), Kansas
1892 60	Residence	1892 Luther (Clay), Kansas
1892 60	Death	02 Jun 1892 Dunlap (Morris), Kansas; Age: 60
1892 60	Burial	Aft. 02 Jun 1892 Dunlap (Morris), Kansas
	Genealogy	Lois Ellen Fenn, The Northwestern Leatherwoods, 1977.
	Occupation-1	farmer; Planter
	Political	Morris County, Kansas; Justice of the Peace

Kinship Report for Joseph D. Leatherwood

Name:	Birth Date:	Relationship:
Albaugh, Nancy Rebecca	19 Nov 1871	Wife of nephew
Auckerman, Aaron J.	29 Jan 1872	Nephew
Auckerman, Anna Lee	18 Nov 1887	Niece
Auckerman, Bessie Mae	12 Sep 1884	Niece
Auckerman, Elsie Ora	14 Oct 1873	Niece
Auckerman, Florence G.	25 Sep 1870	Niece
Auckerman, Jacob C.	Nov 1868	Nephew
Auckerman, John	Mar 1882	Nephew
Auckerman, Katie	Sep 1880	Niece
Auckerman, Minnie Maud	21 Apr 1878	Niece
Auckerman, Truman J.	29 Dec 1879	Nephew
Auckerman, Walter Ray	23 May 1883	Nephew
Auckerman, William	30 Jul 1838	Brother-in-law
Auckerman, William	10 Feb 1876	Nephew
Bangs, Martha	Sep 1853	Wife of 1st cousin
Bauman, Tressa	Abt. 1887	Wife of nephew
Beadles, William E.		Husband of aunt
Beaver, Elizabeth Anna	16 Sep 1780	Maternal grandmother
Beekman, Mahala	Abt. 1816	Wife of uncle
Bennett, William		Brother-in-law
Boll, Wallace Luke	09 May 1901	Husband of granddaughter
Brooks, Estella Harriet	05 Sep 1872	Wife of nephew
Cannon, Montier B.	01 Jan 1846	Husband of niece
Clark, Dennis		Son-in-law
Clark, Elizabeth E.	26 Jan 1846	Wife of 1st cousin
Collins, Charles A.	30 May 1864	Nephew
Collins, Dollie Mae	30 Oct 1874	Niece
Collins, Dora B.	18 Aug 1877	Niece
Collins, Elizabeth Sophia	05 Mar 1867	Niece
Collins, Frederic	Abt. 1872	Nephew
Collins, Jeanette "Nettie'	11 Jul 1869	Niece
Collins, John W.	19 Jul 1861	Nephew
Collins, Theodore S.F.	15 Nov 1829	Brother-in-law
Dale, Sarah	Oct 1846	Wife of 1st cousin
Davidson, Matilda	09 Mar 1845	Wife of 1st cousin
Drake, Miranda Mae	17 Nov 1877	Wife of nephew

Name:	Birth Date:	Relationship:
Dunlap, Henrietta "Hester"	Abt. 1828	Wife of uncle
Eagle, Mabel Ellen	29 Jul 1918	Wife of grandson
Fenn, Francis William	29 Jul 1869	Son-in-law
Fenn, Infant Daughter	Abt. 1896	Granddaughter
Fenn, Infant son	Abt. 1892	Grandson
Fenn, Lois Ellen	23 Jan 1899	Granddaughter
Ferris, Alonzo J.	Abt. 1861	Husband of niece
Fisk, Saretta May	18 Oct 1904	Wife of grandson
Fuller, Elsie Viola	14 Aug 1888	Wife of grandson
Gendron, Arthene Dorothy	31 Mar 1914	Wife of grandson
Graham, Byron Henry Senior	30 Aug 1895	Husband of granddaughter
Grimes, Irving	1875	Husband of niece
Hadley, Cornelius Nathan Junior	11 Apr 1898	Husband of granddaughter
Hamilton, Andrew	Abt. 1810	Uncle
Hamilton, Elizabeth	22 Jan 1813	Mother
Hamilton, William Harrison	24 Aug 1778	Maternal grandfather
Hammond, Benjamin Huge	1844	Husband of 1st cousin
Hammond, Bruce Oscar	27 Sep 1852	Brother-in-law
Hammond, Maud Flora	24 Aug 1877	Niece
Hammond, Oscar Orton	30 Dec 1879	Nephew
Hammond, Rosalie	04 Jul 1888	Niece
Hampshire, Hannah H.	Nov 1825	Wife of uncle
Hatfield, Mary Catherine	29 Aug 1855	Wife of 1st cousin
Hatfield, Sarah Elizabeth	18 Mar 1854	Wife of 1st cousin
Hayden, Helen	20 Dec 1862	Wife of nephew
Heathman, George Everett Junior	05 Aug 1881	Husband of granddaughter
Hibbs, Dorothy J.	17 Sep 1846	Wife of 1st cousin
Hill, Sherman Mentor	21 Nov 1866	Husband of niece
Holcomb, Nita Pearl	Abt. 1880	Daughter-in-law
Irvin, Katherine "Kassie"	1868	Wife of 1st cousin
Jones, Emma J.	27 Sep 1883	Daughter-in-law
Kaufman, Alice Ethel	Abt. 1904	Wife of grandson
Klemper, John A.	Abt. 1885	Husband of niece
La Forest, Ernest T.	1902	Husband of granddaughter
Leatherwood, Aaron	10 Sep 1806	Father
Leatherwood, Amanda	27 Feb 1896	Granddaughter
Leatherwood, America Belle "Meek"	17 Feb 1844	Sister

Name:	Birth Date:	Relationship:
Leatherwood, Anna M.	15 Dec 1862	Daughter
Leatherwood, Chester Boyd	06 Nov 1911	Grandson
Leatherwood, David Edward	Mar 1853	Paternal 1st cousin
Leatherwood, Dorothy Marie	04 Jan 1907	Granddaughter
Leatherwood, Edith Joy	14 Nov 1910	Granddaughter
Leatherwood, Edna May	14 Jul 1898	Granddaughter
Leatherwood, Eliza	Sep 1803	Aunt
Leatherwood, Elizabeth	10 Mar 1891	Granddaughter
Leatherwood, Elizabeth Corilla	Abt. 1847	Paternal 1st cousin
Leatherwood, Elmer O.	04 Sep 1872	Nephew
Leatherwood, Elva	Abt. 1863	Paternal 1st cousin
Leatherwood, Emily Katherine	15 Nov 1883	Granddaughter
Leatherwood, Emma	Jun 1851	Wife of 1st cousin
Leatherwood, Euphema	1803	Aunt
Leatherwood, Hannah Elizabeth	11 Feb 1861	Daughter
Leatherwood, Harlan Price	17 Oct 1904	Grandson
Leatherwood, Henry J.	Jun 1845	Paternal 1st cousin
Leatherwood, Hester Anna	05 Feb 1854	Paternal 1st cousin
Leatherwood, James C.	Abt. 1847	Paternal 1st cousin
Leatherwood, James Robert	06 Aug 1886	Grandson
Leatherwood, John Wesley	Abt. 1810	Uncle
Leatherwood, Joseph Alonzo	05 Jan 1885	Grandson
Leatherwood, Joseph D.	23 Dec 1831	Self
Leatherwood, Joseph Fink	1852	Paternal 1st cousin
Leatherwood, Joseph Harlan	20 May 1874	Son
Leatherwood, Joshua	Abt. 1816	Uncle
Leatherwood, Kathryn Ramona	10 May 1899	Granddaughter
Leatherwood, Leah Elizabeth "Betsy"	22 Nov 1835	Sister
Leatherwood, Lewis D.	May 1860	Paternal 1st cousin
Leatherwood, Mabel Maude	20 Aug 1917	Granddaughter
Leatherwood, Macy Edwin	16 Sep 1869	Son
Leatherwood, Martha J. "Jennie"	Aug 1848	Sister
Leatherwood, Mary Catherine "Katie"	23 Apr 1864	Paternal 1st cousin
Leatherwood, Mary Elizabeth	23 Mar 1846	Sister
Leatherwood, Miranda	Abt. 1823	Aunt
Leatherwood, Nancy Catherine "Kate"	Abt. 1841	Sister
Leatherwood, Nathaniel M.	19 Aug 1822	Uncle

Name:	Birth Date:	Relationship:
Leatherwood, Reuhama	Abt. 1813	Aunt
Leatherwood, Robert Carroll	10 Sep 1908	Grandson
Leatherwood, Roscoe Aaron	09 Feb 1872	Son
Leatherwood, Roscoe Harlan	06 Aug 1900	Grandson
Leatherwood, Russell Keith	27 Oct 1907	Grandson
Leatherwood, Ruth	Abt. 1820	Aunt
Leatherwood, Ruth	14 Apr 1894	Granddaughter
Leatherwood, Samuel	Abt. 1838	Brother
Leatherwood, Samuel	Abt. 1862	Paternal 1st cousin
Leatherwood, Samuel Townsend	09 Sep 1866	Son
Leatherwood, Tamzen Jane	25 Oct 1888	Granddaughter
Leatherwood, Tamzen Jane "Tammie"	01 Feb 1858	Daughter
Leatherwood, Walter William	05 Mar 1852	Paternal 1st cousin
Leatherwood, William Franklin	20 Aug 1903	Grandson
Leatherwood, William Hamilton	07 Sep 1839	Brother
Leatherwood, William R. "Willy"	07 Jun 1859	Son
Leatherwood, Zachariah	18 Jan 1779	Paternal grandfather
Lewis, Augustus	1848	Paternal 1st cousin
Lewis, James	1842	Paternal 1st cousin
Lewis, Laben	1810	Husband of aunt
Lewis, Unidentified daughter - 2	Abt. 1839	Paternal 1st cousin
Lewis, Unidentified daughter -1	Abt. 1837	Paternal 1st cousin
Losey, William	1887	Husband of niece
McCracken, Leona	25 Jul 1886	Wife of nephew
McShane, Francis Thomas	20 Nov 1895	Husband of granddaughter
Merrick, Dora E.	Abt. 1884	Wife of nephew
Mustard, Oscar Leon	24 Mar 1870	Husband of niece
Neese, William		Husband of aunt
Nichols, Emily Pleasant	13 Jan 1833	Wife
Palmer, Daniel J.	Abt. 1843	Brother-in-law
Phillips, Henry Herschel	03 Jan 1879	Husband of niece
Polster, Edward W.	08 Mar 1882	Husband of niece
Price, Edith May	29 Dec 1876	Daughter-in-law
Ratliff, Everett Ambrose	03 Jul 1891	Husband of granddaughter
Rinehart, John	Jul 1860	Husband of 1st cousin
Rivers, Gertrude Aphia	19 Nov 1900	Wife of grandson
Rowen, Narcissa	14 Mar 1848	Wife of 1st cousin

Name:	Birth Date:	Relationship:
Rowney, Harold Joseph	25 Nov 1909	Husband of granddaughter
Ryman, America Elizabeth	08 Dec 1860	Daughter-in-law
Schaeffer, Amelia Jane "Minnie"	06 Mar 1849	Wife of 1st cousin
Setty, Sanford Enoch	04 Aug 1848	Husband of 1st cousin
Sheaffer, Harriet Emily "Hattie"	11 Nov 1859	Wife of 1st cousin
Smith, Charles Howard	1864	Husband of niece
Smith, E. E.		Brother-in-law
Smith, Lillian Edith	23 Feb 1884	Niece
Smith, Walter Ray	Apr 1889	Nephew
Stanford, Irene Beatrice	20 Jul 1906	Wife of grandson
Stewart, Sylvan Leslie	27 Aug 1892	Husband of granddaughter
Tener, Catherine	Abt. 1777	Paternal grandmother
Thomas, Susan Sarah	26 Oct 1867	Daughter-in-law
Thompson, Clyde Arlington	20 Apr 1892	Husband of granddaughter
Wilson, Mary Armintha	15 Sep 1872	Wife of 1st cousin
Zink, Aaron Russell	26 Nov 1837	Paternal 1st cousin
Zink, Daniel Z.	20 Sep 1839	Paternal 1st cousin
Zink, Elizabeth Corilla	05 Dec 1834	Paternal 1st cousin
Zink, Joseph Bittler	25 May 1849	Paternal 1st cousin
Zink, Nathaniel McClure	05 Nov 1843	Paternal 1st cousin
Zink, Philip Jacob Senior	25 Jul 1800	Husband of aunt
Zink, Philip Jacob Junior	21 Apr 1842	Paternal 1st cousin
Zink, Samuel James	29 May 1836	Paternal 1st cousin
Zink, William Hanby	12 May 1846	Paternal 1st cousin

Ancestors of Joseph D. Leatherwood

Generation 1

1. **Joseph D. Leatherwood**, son of Aaron Leatherwood and Elizabeth Hamilton, was born on 23 Dec 1831 in Sinking Springs (Highland), Ohio. He died on 02 Jun 1892 in Dunlap (Morris), Kansas (Age: 60). He married **Emily Pleasant Nichols** on 09 Oct 1856 in Adams County, Ohio. She was born on 13 Jan 1833 in Loudoun County, Virginia. She died on 13 Sep 1882 in Dunlap (Morris), Kansas.

Generation 2

2. **Aaron Leatherwood**, son of Zachariah Leatherwood and Catherine Tener, was born on 10 Sep 1806 in Frederick County, Maryland. He died on 21 Jul 1891 in Locust Grove (Adams), Ohio (Age: 84). He married **Elizabeth Hamilton** on 13 Jan 1831 in Locust Grove (Adams), Ohio.

3. **Elizabeth Hamilton**, daughter of William Harrison Hamilton and Elizabeth Anna Beaver, was born on 22 Jan 1813 in Meigs (Adams), Ohio. She died on 03 May 1858 in Locust Grove (Adams), Ohio (Age: 45).

Elizabeth Hamilton and Aaron Leatherwood had the following children:

1.   i.   Joseph D. Leatherwood was born on 23 Dec 1831 in Sinking Springs (Highland), Ohio. He died on 02 Jun 1892 in Dunlap (Morris), Kansas (Age: 60). He married Emily Pleasant Nichols on 09 Oct 1856 in Adams County, Ohio. She was born on 13 Jan 1833 in Loudoun County, Virginia. She died on 13 Sep 1882 in Dunlap (Morris), Kansas.

      ii.   Leah Elizabeth "Betsy" Leatherwood was born on 22 Nov 1835 in Locust Grove (Adams), Ohio. She died on 19 Jan 1896 in Lowell (Lake), Indiana. She married Theodore S.F. Collins after 27 Jul 1860 in Adams County, Ohio (It is believed Leah married Theodore Collins during 1860 but after the date cited. The marriage occurred soon after the 1860 census, probably August or September 1860, based on the birth of their first child, John W. Collins, on 19 July 1861.). He was born on 15 Nov 1829 in Ohio. He died on 22 Jul 1892 in Lowell (Lake), Indiana.

      iii.   Samuel Leatherwood was born about 1838 in Locust Grove (Adams), Ohio. He died on 08 Oct 1861 in Cheat Mountain, Virginia (Sergeant Samuel Leatherwood died in a camp hospital from Typhoid fever.).

      iv.   William Hamilton Leatherwood was born on 07 Sep 1839 in Locust Grove (Adams), Ohio. He died on 09 May 1864 in Cloyd's Mountain, Virginia.

      v.   Nancy Catherine "Kate" Leatherwood was born about 1841 in Locust Grove (Adams), Ohio. She died on 25 Mar 1911 in Paint (Highland), Ohio. She married William Auckerman about 1867 in Adams County, Ohio. He was born on 30 Jul 1838 in Lawrence County, Ohio. He died on 03 Feb 1912 in Dayton (Montgomery), Ohio.

      vi.   America Belle "Meek" Leatherwood was born on 17 Feb 1844 in Locust Grove (Adams), Ohio. She died on 04 Sep 1906 in Salt Lake City (Salt Lake), Utah (Age: 62). She married William Bennett. He was born in Pike County, Ohio.

      vii.   Mary Elizabeth Leatherwood was born on 23 Mar 1846 in Locust Grove (Adams), Ohio. She died on 12 Sep 1926 in Franklin (Adams), Ohio. She married Daniel J. Palmer about 1907 in Adams County, Ohio. He was born about 1843 in Ohio. She married Bruce Oscar Hammond about 1877 in Adams County, Ohio. He was born on 27 Sep 1852 in Ohio. He died on 17 Dec 1893 in Adams County, Ohio.

      viii.   Martha J. "Jennie" Leatherwood was born in Aug 1848 in Adams County, Ohio. She married E. E. Smith.

4. **Zachariah Leatherwood**, son of Samuel Leatherwood III and Hannah Delphy Buckingham, was born on 18 Jan 1779 in Frederick (Frederick), Maryland. He died on 23 Sep 1850 in Adams County, Ohio. He married **Catherine Tener** on 19 Sep 1802 in Baltimore County, Maryland (Alternate date cited: 17 Nov 1802).

5. **Catherine Tener**, daughter of John Tener and Margaret Dorsey, was born about 1777 in Baltimore (Baltimore), Maryland. She died about 1853 in Adams County, Ohio.

   Catherine Tener and Zachariah Leatherwood had the following children:

       i.   Euphema Leatherwood was born in 1803 in Frederick County, Maryland.

       ii.   Eliza Leatherwood was born in Sep 1803 in Frederick County, Maryland. She died on 14 Mar 1890 in Union Star (DeKalb), Missouri. She married William Neese. She married Philip Jacob Zink Senior on 19 Dec 1833 in Highland County, Ohio (Recorded 29 December 1833.). He was born on 25 Jul 1800 in Shenandoah County, Virginia. He died on 19 Oct 1854 in Galesburg (Knox), Illinois. She married William E. Beadles on 12 Nov 1887 in Indiana.

2.   iii. Aaron Leatherwood was born on 10 Sep 1806 in Frederick County, Maryland. He died on 21 Jul 1891 in Locust Grove (Adams), Ohio (Age: 84). He married Elizabeth Hamilton on 13 Jan 1831 in Locust Grove (Adams), Ohio. She was born on 22 Jan 1813 in Meigs (Adams), Ohio. She died on 03 May 1858 in Locust Grove (Adams), Ohio (Age: 45).

       iv. John Wesley Leatherwood was born about 1810 in Frederick County, Maryland. He died on 21 Jul 1891 in Locust Grove (Adams), Ohio. He married Hannah H. Hampshire on 18 Dec 1845 in Pike County, Ohio. She was born in Nov 1825 in Ohio ( ). She died on 04 Oct 1909 in Washington (Fayette), Ohio.

       v.   Reuhama Leatherwood was born about 1813 in Frederick County, Maryland. She married Laben Lewis on 17 Feb 1836 in Highland, Ohio, USA. He was born in 1810.

       vi. Joshua Leatherwood was born about 1816 in Frederick County, Maryland. He died about 1834 in Highland County, Ohio.

      vii. Ruth Leatherwood was born about 1820 in Frederick County, Maryland.

     viii. Nathaniel M. Leatherwood was born on 19 Aug 1822 in Adams County, Ohio. He died on 18 Nov 1864 in Saint Louis (Saint Louis) Missouri. He married Henrietta "Hester" Dunlap in 1844. She was born about 1828 in Ohio. She died on 23 May 1864 in Pike County, Ohio.

       ix. Miranda Leatherwood was born about 1823 in Adams County, Ohio.

6. **William Harrison Hamilton**, son of Thomas Hamilton and Nancy Ann UMN Hamilton, was born on 24 Aug 1778 in Cynthiana (Harrison), Kentucky. He died on 22 Dec 1857 in Franklin Township (Adams), Ohio. He married **Elizabeth Anna Beaver** on 31 Jan 1803 in Bourbon (Harrison), Kentucky.

7. **Elizabeth Anna Beaver** was born on 16 Sep 1780 in Harrison County, Kentucky. She died on 13 Jan 1858 in Adams County, Ohio.

   Elizabeth Anna Beaver and William Harrison Hamilton had the following children:

       i.   Andrew Hamilton was born about 1810. He married Mahala Beekman. She was born about 1816. She died in Jan 1842 in Adams County, Ohio.

3.   ii.   Elizabeth Hamilton was born on 22 Jan 1813 in Meigs (Adams), Ohio. She died on 03 May 1858 in Locust Grove (Adams), Ohio (Age: 45). She married Aaron Leatherwood on 13 Jan 1831 in Locust Grove (Adams), Ohio. He was born on 10

Sep 1806 in Frederick County, Maryland. He died on 21 Jul 1891 in Locust Grove (Adams), Ohio (Age: 84).

Generation 4

8. **Samuel Leatherwood III**, son of Samuel Leatherwood II and Francis Buckingham, was born about 1754 in Carroll County, Maryland (HIs birth place is cited as Carroll County, Maryland but Carroll County, Maryland was not created until 1837. He was probably born in Baltimore County, the portion that became Carroll County.). He died on 29 May 1821 in Caleb's Delight (Carroll), Maryland. He married **Hannah Delphy Buckingham** on 08 Aug 1778 in Frederick County, Maryland.

9. **Hannah Delphy Buckingham**, daughter of Benjamin Buckingham Senior and Avarilla Gosnell, was born in 1750 in Frederick (Frederick), Maryland. She died on 30 Aug 1842 in Frederick (Frederick), Maryland (Age: 92).

Hannah Delphy Buckingham and Samuel Leatherwood III had the following children:

4.   i.   Zachariah Leatherwood was born on 18 Jan 1779 in Frederick (Frederick), Maryland. He died on 23 Sep 1850 in Adams County, Ohio. He married Catherine Tener on 19 Sep 1802 in Baltimore County, Maryland (Alternate date cited: 17 Nov 1802). She was born about 1777 in Baltimore (Baltimore), Maryland. She died about 1853 in Adams County, Ohio.

   ii.   Mary Leatherwood was born on 14 Jun 1780 in Frederick (Frederick), Maryland. She died on 25 Jun 1871 in Carroll County, Maryland. She married Hamlet Gilliss on 22 Apr 1806 in Baltimore County, Maryland. He was born on 02 Mar 1774 in Baltimore County, Maryland. He died on 25 Mar 1837 in Baltimore County, Maryland.

   iii.   John Leatherwood was born on 26 Sep 1782 in Franklinville (Frederick), Maryland. He died in Jun 1850 in Gosnell (Carroll), Maryland. He married Elizabeth Gilliss on 24 Dec 1809 in Baltimore County, Maryland. She was born on 24 Aug 1792 in Baltimore County, Maryland. She died on 18 Nov 1813 in Baltimore County, Maryland. He married Mrs. John Leatherwood about 1804. She was born in 1785 in Maryland. She died about 1809 in Maryland. He married Elizabeth Cushen on 07 Jul 1815 in Baltimore County, Maryland. She was born on 24 Oct 1790 in Baltimore County, Maryland. She died on 26 Feb 1871 in Freedom (Carroll), Maryland.

   iv.   Elizabeth Leatherwood was born on 21 Nov 1784 in Frederick (Frederick), Maryland. She died before 15 Mar 1850 in Frederick County, Maryland. She married John Fowler on 15 Dec 1810 in Frederick County, Maryland. He was born about 1780 in Maryland.

   v.   Apparilla Leatherwood was born on 30 Jun 1785 in Frederick (Frederick), Maryland. She died on 28 Jun 1871 in Carroll County, Maryland. She married John Butler on 02 Feb 1820 in Frederick County, Maryland. He was born on 05 Mar 1795 in Maryland. He died on 28 Feb 1867 in Carroll County, Maryland.

   vi.   Ruth Leatherwood was born on 08 Nov 1787 in Frederick (Frederick), Maryland.

   vii.   Rachel Leatherwood was born on 30 Oct 1790 in Frederick (Frederick), Maryland. She died in 1870 in Montgomery County, Maryland. She married Rezin Mullinix on 04 Jan 1819 in Frederick County, Maryland. He was born about 1798 in Maryland.

   viii.   Nellie Leatherwood was born on 04 Jul 1793 in Frederick (Frederick), Maryland.

10. **John Tener**, son of William Tener and Ann Maynard, was born on 13 Apr 1725 in Luxenburg (Bad Salsungen), Germany. He died on 13 Apr 1804 in Carroll County, Maryland (Age: 79). He married **Margaret Dorsey**.

11. **Margaret Dorsey**, daughter of Edward Dorsey, was born in 1731. She died in 1806.

Margaret Dorsey and John Tener had the following children:

    i.   Phillp Tener was born about 1755 in Maryland. He died about 1833 in Maryland. He married Elizabeth Clay on 31 Dec 1808 in Maryland.

    ii.   Henry Tener was born about 1757 in Maryland. He died about 1785 in Maryland. He married Hester ULN.

    iii.   George Tener was born about 1764 in Maryland. He died on 09 Jul 1838. He married an unknown spouse on 17 Mar 1810 in Baltimore (Baltimore), Maryland.

    iv.   Jacob Tener was born about 1766 in Maryland. He died on 17 Sep 1845 in Adams County, Ohio. He married Catherine Porter on 19 Sep 1797 in Maryland.

    v.   Adam Tener was born about 1770 in Maryland. He died about 1850. He married an unknown spouse on 23 Mar 1805 in Frederick County, Maryland.

    vi.   Margaret Tener was born about 1774 in Maryland. She died about 1840. She married Joshua Porter Jr. on 06 Apr 1799 in Baltimore County, Maryland.

5.   vii.   Catherine Tener was born about 1777 in Baltimore (Baltimore), Maryland. She died about 1853 in Adams County, Ohio. She married Zachariah Leatherwood on 19 Sep 1802 in Baltimore County, Maryland (Alternate date cited: 17 Nov 1802). He was born on 18 Jan 1779 in Frederick (Frederick), Maryland. He died on 23 Sep 1850 in Adams County, Ohio.

12. **Thomas Hamilton** was born about 1750 in Virginia. He married **Nancy Ann UMN Hamilton**.

13. **Nancy Ann UMN Hamilton** was born in 1746 in Newville (Cumberland), Pennsylvania. She died in 1795.

Nancy Ann UMN Hamilton and Thomas Hamilton had the following child:

6.   i.   William Harrison Hamilton was born on 24 Aug 1778 in Cynthiana (Harrison), Kentucky. He died on 22 Dec 1857 in Franklin Township (Adams), Ohio. He married Elizabeth Anna Beaver on 31 Jan 1803 in Bourbon (Harrison), Kentucky. She was born on 16 Sep 1780 in Harrison County, Kentucky. She died on 13 Jan 1858 in Adams County, Ohio.

Generation 5

16. **Samuel Leatherwood II**, son of Samuel Leatherwood I and Johanna Young, was born on 11 Feb 1722 in Anne Arundel County, Maryland. He died on 14 Feb 1788 in Frederick County, Maryland. He married **Francis Buckingham** about 1741 in Anne Arundel County, Maryland.

17. **Francis Buckingham**, daughter of John Buckingham and Hannah Gosnell, was born on 27 Nov 1723 in Anne Arundel County, Maryland. She died in 1797 in Frederick (Frederick), Maryland (Sources range from 1788 to 1797).

Francis Buckingham and Samuel Leatherwood II had the following children:

    i.   Elizabeth Urath Leatherwood was born on 26 Jan 1743 in Anne Arundel County, Maryland. She married an unknown spouse on 31 Oct 1778 in Baltimore County, Maryland.

    ii.   Thomas Leatherwood was born on 23 Aug 1743 in Anne Arundel County, Maryland. He died on 29 Nov 1811 in Anne Arundel County, Maryland (Heirs & Orphans: Anne Arundel County, Maryland Distributions, 1788-1838, compiled by Walter E. Arps, Jr., (Westminster, Md.: Willow Bend Books, 1992), page (s) 41.). He married Mary Porter on 31 Jan 1784 in Baltimore (Baltimore), Maryland. She was born about 1751. She died on 17 Nov 1821 in Elk Ridge (Anne Arundel), Maryland.

    iii.   Delila Leatherwood was born about 1744 in Anne Arundel County, Maryland. She married William Wilson. He was born about 1744 in Limrick, Ireland.

    iv.   John Leatherwood was born about 1746 in Anne Arundel County, Maryland.

    v.   Mary Ann Leatherwood was born about 1752 in Anne Arundel County, Maryland. She died on 20 Apr 1841 in Violet (Fairfield), Ohio. She married John G. Buckingham about 1775 in Maryland. He was born on 06 Mar 1748 in Saint (Thomas) Baltimore, Maryland. He died in Aug 1828 in Muskingum (Muskinggum), Ohio.

8.   vi.   Samuel Leatherwood III was born about 1754 in Carroll County, Maryland (HIs birth place is cited as Carroll County, Maryland but Carroll County, Maryland was not created until 1837. He was probably born in Baltimore County, the portion that became Carroll County.). He died on 29 May 1821 in Caleb's Delight (Carroll), Maryland. He married Hannah Delphy Buckingham on 08 Aug 1778 in Frederick County, Maryland. She was born in 1750 in Frederick (Frederick), Maryland. She died on 30 Aug 1842 in Frederick (Frederick), Maryland (Age: 92).

    vii.   Rachel Leatherwood was born about 1754 in Carroll County, Maryland. She married Benjamin Buckingham Junior. He was born about 1745 in Maryland.

    viii.   Sarah Anne Leatherwood was born about 1754 in Anne Arundel County, Maryland. She died about 1848. She married John Dicas on 03 Jan 1778 in Baltimore County, Maryland (Baltimore County Marriage Licenses, 1777-1798, compiled by Dawn Beitler Smith, (Westminister, Md.: Family Line Publications, 1989), page (s) 113./Baltimore (Baltimore), Maryland). He was born in 1755. He died in 1783.

    ix.   Ann Leatherwood was born about 1759 in Carroll County, Maryland. She married Nichel Hewitt on 07 Sep 1779 in Baltimore County, Maryland (Baltimore County Marriage Licenses, 1777-1798, compiled by Dawn Beitler Smith, (Westminister, Md. - Family Line Publications, 1989), page (s) 113.).

    x.   Ruth Leatherwood was born about 1760 in Frederick County, Maryland. She married Nathan Buckingham Senior on 16 Jun 1792 in Baltimore (Baltimore), Maryland. He was born about 1740 in Maryland. He died in 1815.

    xi.   Frances Leatherwood was born about 1762 in Frederick County, Maryland. She died on 02 Apr 1854 in Oxford (Guernsey), Ohio. She married Anthony Arnold. He was born in 1761 in Pennsylvania. He died on 19 Sep 1823 in Guernsey County, Ohio. She married an unknown spouse on 22 Aug 1782 in Frederick County, Maryland.

    xii.   Nancy Leatherwood was born on abt 1747 - died young.

18.   **Benjamin Buckingham Senior**, son of John Buckingham and Hannah Gosnell, was born on 12 Mar 1721 in Anne Arundel County, Maryland. He died on 03 Dec 1800 in Baltimore County, Maryland. He married **Avarilla Gosnell** in Maryland.

19.   **Avarilla Gosnell**, daughter of William Gosnell and Elizabeth Nash, was born in Sep 1720 in Baltimore (Baltimore), Maryland.

Avarilla Gosnell and Benjamin Buckingham Senior had the following children:

    i.   Nathan Buckingham Senior was born about 1740 in Maryland. He died in 1815. He married Ruth Leatherwood on 16 Jun 1792 in Baltimore (Baltimore), Maryland. She was born about 1760 in Frederick County, Maryland. He married Esther Osborn in 1763. She was born in 1743 in Connecticut. She died on 18 Dec 1813.

    ii.   Benjamin Buckingham Junior was born about 1745 in Maryland. He married Rachel Leatherwood. She was born about 1754 in Carroll County, Maryland.

    iii.   William Buckingham was born about 1747 in Baltimore (Baltimore), Maryland.

	iv.	John Buckingham was born on 06 Mar 1748 in Baltimore (Baltimore), Maryland.

9.   v.   Hannah Delphy Buckingham was born in 1750 in Frederick (Frederick), Maryland. She died on 30 Aug 1842 in Frederick (Frederick), Maryland (Age: 92). She married Samuel Leatherwood III on 08 Aug 1778 in Frederick County, Maryland. He was born about 1754 in Carroll County, Maryland (HIs birth place is cited as Carroll County, Maryland but Carroll County, Maryland was not created until 1837. He was probably born in Baltimore County, the portion that became Carroll County.). He died on 29 May 1821 in Caleb's Delight (Carroll), Maryland.

      vi.   Ann Buckingham was born about 1750 in Baltimore (Baltimore), Maryland.

      vii.   Emily Buckingham was born about 1755 in Maryland.

      viii.   Emily Buckingham was born about 1755 in Maryland.

      ix.   Obediah Buckingham was born on 03 Oct 1757 in Baltimore County, Maryland. He died on 03 Apr 1839 in Baltimore County, Maryland. He married Ruth Heddington on 23 Oct 1784 in Baltimore County, Maryland. She was born in 1754 in Maryland. She died on 18 Dec 1843 in Westminster (Carroll), Maryland.

20.   **William Tener**, son of Charles Turner and Mary Cockey (Tener Turner), was born on 17 Feb 1704 in Anne Arundel County, Maryland. He died on 11 Jul 1752 in Frederick County, Maryland. He married **Ann Maynard**.

21.   **Ann Maynard** was born about 1697 in Anne Arundel, Maryland, USA. She died before 17 Mar 1749 in Frederick County, Maryland, USA.

Ann Maynard and William Tener had the following child:

10.   i.   John Tener was born on 13 Apr 1725 in Luxenburg (Bad Salsungen), Germany. He died on 13 Apr 1804 in Carroll County, Maryland (Age: 79). He married Margaret Dorsey. She was born in 1731. She died in 1806.

22.   **Edward Dorsey** was born in 1710 in Maryland.

Edward Dorsey had the following child:

11.   i.   Margaret Dorsey was born in 1731. She died in 1806. She married John Tener. He was born on 13 Apr 1725 in Luxenburg (Bad Salsungen), Germany. He died on 13 Apr 1804 in Carroll County, Maryland (Age: 79).

Generation 6

32.   **Samuel Leatherwood I**, son of John Leatherwood and Martha "Mollie" Kitteu, was born on 13 Feb 1681 in Annapolis (Anne Arundel), Maryland. He died about 1754 in Annapolis (Anne Arundel), Maryland. He married **Johanna Young** about 1712 in Maryland.

33.   **Johanna Young**, daughter of John Young and Elizabeth Sewell, was born between 1686-1690 in Anne Arundel County, Maryland. She died in Maryland.

Johanna Young and Samuel Leatherwood I had the following children:

      i.   John Leatherwood was born on 08 Apr 1714 in Baltimore County, Maryland. He died on 29 Nov 1794 in Dettingen Parish (Prince William), Virginia. He married Sarah Sally Hunt about 1735 in Prince William County, Virginia. She was born in Jan 1720 in Virginia. She died about 1765 in Dettingen Parish (Prince William), Virginia.

      ii.   Martha Leatherwood was born on 30 Jan 1716 in Annapolis (Anne Arundel), Maryland. She died in 1737 in Anne Arundel County, Maryland. She married Samuel Shipley on 21 Oct 1734 in Anne Arundel County, Maryland. He was born about 1710 in Anne Arundel County, Maryland. He died about 1780 in Howard County, Maryland.

iii. Nathan Leatherwood was born on 29 Jul 1717 in Annapolis (Anne Arundel), Maryland. He died.

iv. Rachell Leatherwood was born on 30 Mar 1720 in Annapolis (Anne Arundel), Maryland.

16. v. Samuel Leatherwood II was born on 11 Feb 1722 in Anne Arundel County, Maryland. He died on 14 Feb 1788 in Frederick County, Maryland. He married Francis Buckingham about 1741 in Anne Arundel County, Maryland. She was born on 27 Nov 1723 in Anne Arundel County, Maryland. She died in 1797 in Frederick (Frederick), Maryland (Sources range from 1788 to 1797).

vi. Jemima "Jeminor" Leatherwood was born on 04 Jan 1729 in Anne Arundel County, Maryland. She married William Pickett on 13 Dec 1777 in Baltimore (Baltimore), Maryland. She married Deaver.

vii. Zachariah Leatherwood was born about 1730 in Annapolis (Anne Arundel), Maryland.

viii. Mary Leatherwood was born on 11 Nov 1735 in Anne Arundel County, Maryland.

34. **John Buckingham**, son of John Buckingham and Francis Cooper, was born on 28 Oct 1700 in Anne Arundel County, Maryland (Recorded in St. Margaret's Parish/). He died on 03 Dec 1741 in Anne Arundel County, Maryland (Recorded in St. Margaret's Parish/). He married **Hannah Gosnell** on 31 Jan 1720 in Annapolis (Anne Arundel), Maryland (Recorded at St. Anne's Parish).

35. **Hannah Gosnell**, daughter of William Gosnell and Sarah Baker, was born between 1692-1700 in Anne Arundel County, Maryland. She died about 1741 in Baltimore (Baltimore), Maryland.

Hannah Gosnell and John Buckingham had the following children:

i. Thomas Buckingham was born about 1720 in Anne Arundel County, Maryland. He died about 1754 in Chester, Pennsylvania.

18. ii. Benjamin Buckingham Senior was born on 12 Mar 1721 in Anne Arundel County, Maryland. He died on 03 Dec 1800 in Baltimore County, Maryland. He married Avarilla Gosnell in Maryland. She was born in Sep 1720 in Baltimore (Baltimore), Maryland.

iii. Anne Buckingham was born on 08 Nov 1722 in Anne Arundel County, Maryland.

17. iv. Francis Buckingham was born on 27 Nov 1723 in Anne Arundel County, Maryland. She died in 1797 in Frederick (Frederick), Maryland (Sources range from 1788 to 1797). She married Samuel Leatherwood II about 1741 in Anne Arundel County, Maryland. He was born on 11 Feb 1722 in Anne Arundel County, Maryland. He died on 14 Feb 1788 in Frederick County, Maryland.

v. Lavina Buckingham was born on 08 Feb 1727 in Anne Arundel County, Maryland. She died on 31 May 1729 in Anne Arundel County, Maryland.

vi. John Buckingham was born about 1730 in Anne Arundel County, Maryland. He died before 03 Dec 1800 in Baltimore (Baltimore), Maryland.

38. **William Gosnell**, son of William Gosnell and Sarah Baker, was born about 1698 in Anne Arundel County, Maryland. He died about 1762 in Baltimore (Baltimore), Maryland. He married **Elizabeth Nash** about 1718 in Anne Arundel County, Maryland.

39. **Elizabeth Nash**, daughter of William Naish and Sarah Elizabeth Baker, was born about 1694 in Anne Arundel County, Maryland. She died in 1752 in Baltimore (Baltimore), Maryland.

Elizabeth Nash and William Gosnell had the following children:

19. i. Avarilla Gosnell was born in Sep 1720 in Baltimore (Baltimore), Maryland. She married Benjamin Buckingham Senior in Maryland. He was born on 12 Mar 1721 in

Anne Arundel County, Maryland. He died on 03 Dec 1800 in Baltimore County, Maryland.

ii. John Gosnell.

40. **Charles Turner** was born in 1675 in Anne Arundel County, Maryland. He died in 1741 in Anne Arundel County, Maryland. He married **Mary Cockey (Tener Turner)**.

41. **Mary Cockey (Tener Turner)** was born on 26 Feb 1672 in Queen Anne Parish (Prince George), Maryland. She died on 26 Nov 1739 in Queen Anne Parish (Prince George), Maryland.

Mary Cockey (Tener Turner) and Charles Turner had the following child:

20. i. William Tener was born on 17 Feb 1704 in Anne Arundel County, Maryland. He died on 11 Jul 1752 in Frederick County, Maryland. He married Ann Maynard. She was born about 1697 in Anne Arundel, Maryland, USA. She died before 17 Mar 1749 in Frederick County, Maryland, USA.

Generation 7

64. **John Leatherwood** was born about 1645 in England. He died in 1716 in Stony Runn (Anne Arundel), Maryland. He married **Martha "Mollie" Kitteu** about 1679 in England.

65. **Martha "Mollie" Kitteu**, daughter of Peter Kitton, was born about 1655 in England. She died on 29 Dec 1704 in Annapolis (Anne Arundel), Maryland.

Martha "Mollie" Kitteu and John Leatherwood had the following children:

i. Mary Leatherwood was born on 12 Aug 1680 in Annapolis (Anne Arundel), Maryland (The date cited is a baptismal data and not neccessarily a birth date.). She died. She married Charles Crane Senior about 1700 in Anne Arundel County, Maryland. He was born in 1675 in Anne Arundel County, Maryland.

32. ii. Samuel Leatherwood I was born on 13 Feb 1681 in Annapolis (Anne Arundel), Maryland. He died about 1754 in Annapolis (Anne Arundel), Maryland. He married Johanna Young about 1712 in Maryland. She was born between 1686-1690 in Anne Arundel County, Maryland. She died in Maryland.

iii. Edward Leatherwood was born on 29 Jan 1685 in Anne Arundel County, Maryland. He married an unknown spouse in 1710 in of, VA.

iv. Johanah (Joanna) Leatherwood was born on 08 Jun 1689 in Annapolis (Anne Arundel), Maryland. She died. She married William Bennett on 10 Jan 1709 in Anne Arundel County, Maryland. He was born on 25 Nov 1684 in Somerset County, Maryland.

v. Jane Leatherwood was born on 08 Mar 1691 in Annapolis (Anne Arundel), Maryland.

vi. Unidentified Daughter Leatherwood was born about 1693 in Annapolis (Anne Arundel), Maryland.

vii. Unidentified Daughter Leatherwood was born about 1695 in Annapolis (Anne Arundel), Maryland.

viii. Unidentified Daughter Leatherwood was born about 1697 in Annapolis (Anne Arundel), Maryland.

ix. Ruth Leatherwood was born about 1699 in Annapolis (Anne Arundel), Maryland. She died.

66. **John Young**, son of Richard Young, was born on 10 Nov 1672 in Brompton (Yorkshire), England. He died in 1741 in Baltimore (Baltimore), Maryland. He married **Elizabeth Sewell** about 1703 in England.

67. **Elizabeth Sewell**, daughter of Henry Sewell II and Johanna Warner, was born about 1675 in

38.   vi.   William Gosnell was born about 1698 in Anne Arundel County, Maryland. He died about 1762 in Baltimore (Baltimore), Maryland. He married Elizabeth Nash about 1718 in Anne Arundel County, Maryland. She was born about 1694 in Anne Arundel County, Maryland. She died in 1752 in Baltimore (Baltimore), Maryland.

78.   **William Naish**. He married **Sarah Elizabeth Baker**.

79.   **Sarah Elizabeth Baker**, daughter of Maurice Baker, was born in 1665 in Anne Arundel County, Maryland. She died in 1710 in Anne Arundel County, Maryland.

Sarah Elizabeth Baker and William Naish had the following child:

39.   i.   Elizabeth Nash was born about 1694 in Anne Arundel County, Maryland. She died in 1752 in Baltimore (Baltimore), Maryland. She married William Gosnell about 1718 in Anne Arundel County, Maryland. He was born about 1698 in Anne Arundel County, Maryland. He died about 1762 in Baltimore (Baltimore), Maryland.

Index